BUDDHISM FOR BEGINNERS

DISCOVER THE PROFOUND WISDOM OF THE BUDDHA'S TEACHINGS AND TRANSFORM YOUR LIFE THROUGH ZEN MEDITATION AND MINDFULNESS PRACTICES

SAMADHI SANDS

Copyrights Notice

No part of this book may be reproduced in any form or by any electronic or mechanical means, including information storage and retrieval systems, without written permission from the author.

Recording of this publication is strictly prohibited and any storage of this document is not allowed unless with written permission from the publisher.

All rights reserved. Respective authors own all copyrights not held by the publisher.

Pictures inside this book are of the respective owners, granted to the Author in a Royalty-Free license.

All trademarks, service marks, product names, and the characteristics of any names mentioned in this book are considered the property of their respective owners and are used only for reference. No endorsement is implied when we use one of these terms.

Limited Liability - Disclaimer

Please note that the content of this book is based on personal experience and various information sources, and it is only for personal use.

Please note the information contained within this document is for educational and entertainment purposes only and no warranties of any kind are declared or implied.

Readers acknowledge that the author is not engaging in the rendering of legal, financial, or professional advice. Please consult a licensed professional before attempting any techniques outlined in this book.

Nothing in this book is intended to replace common sense or legal accounting, or professional advice and is meant only to inform.

Your particular circumstances may not be suited to the example illustrated in this book; in fact, they likely will not be.

You should use the information in this book at your own risk. The reader is responsible for his or her actions.

The information provided herein is stated to be truthful and consistent, in that any liability, in terms of inattention or otherwise, by any usage or abuse of any policies, processes, or directions contained within is the solitary and utter responsibility of the recipient reader.

By reading this book, the reader agrees that under no circumstances is the author responsible for any losses, direct or indirect, which are incurred as a result of the use of the information contained within this document, including, but not limited to, errors, omissions, or inaccuracies.

CONTENTS

Foreword	7
Introduction	9
1. BUDDHISM PHILOSOPHY	17
The Three Universal Truths	17
Annica	18
Dhukka	19
Anatta	19
The Four Noble Truths	20
Dhukka	20
Samudaya	21
Nirodha	22
Magga	23
The Eightfold Path	23
Five Precepts of Buddhism	25
2. SCHOOLS OF BUDDHISM	28
Theravada Buddhism (School of the Elders)	29
Mahayana Buddhism (The Great Vehicle)	29
Zen Buddhism	30
Tibetan Buddhism	32
3. GUIDED BUDDHISM MEDITATION	36
Walking Meditation	36
Mindfulness Meditation	39
Kundalini Yoga	44
What Exactly Are Chakras?	45
The Root Chakra - Muladhara	47
Manipura is the Solar Plexus Chakra	58
Anahata is the Heart Chakra	58
Vishuddha (Throat Chakra)	58
Ajna, the Third Eye Chakra	59
Sahasrara is the Crown Chakra	59

The Importance of Chakra Balancing	60
Healing The Chakra System	60
Transcendental Meditation	64
4. GUIDED TIBETAN MEDITATION	68
Mahamudra Meditation	69
Tummo Meditation	70
Meditation with Tonglen	73
Meditation using Mandalas	76
Meditation on Shamatha	79
Meditation Through Visualization	82
5. GUIDED ZEN MEDITATIONS	86
Meditation at Hua-T'ou	87
Meditation with Koans	90
6. YOGA POSES	94
Yoga Hatha	96
Standing Forward Bend Pose (Uttanasana)	97
(Setu Bandhasana) Bridge Pose	97
Yoga Vinyasa	98
Cat-Cow Pose (Chakravakasana)	99
Salutation to the Sun	99
Yoga for Taoists	100
Bonus Included: 30 Minutes of Guided Meditation	103
About the Author	105

FOREWORD

Dear Reader,

Thank you for choosing to embark on this journey of self-discovery and exploration with "*Buddhism for Beginners: Discover the Profound Wisdom of The Buddha's Teachings and Transform Your Life Through Zen Meditation And Mindfulness Practices.*" We hope that the profound wisdom and transformative practices presented within these pages bring you immense value and inspiration.

While every effort has been made to ensure the utmost accuracy and clarity in the content of this book, we understand that human errors may occasionally occur. In the spirit of continuous improvement, we kindly invite you to participate in this collaborative process.

If you happen to come across any grammar errors or typographical mistakes during your reading, we request your understanding and would be truly grateful if you take a moment to notify us. Your valuable feedback is invaluable and helps us enhance the overall reading experience for all our readers.

FOREWORD

Please feel free to reach out to us via email at samashi.sands@mail.com to point out any corrections, suggestions, or general feedback you may have. We warmly welcome your insights and are committed to addressing any issues promptly.

As authors and publishers, our primary goal is to provide you with the best possible content, and your contribution plays a significant role in achieving that objective. Together, we can strive for greater accuracy, clarity, and overall excellence.

Once again, thank you for your support and for being an essential part of this ongoing endeavor. We sincerely value your participation in making this book an even more valuable resource for all who seek wisdom and transformation through the teachings of Buddhism.

With heartfelt gratitude,

Samadhi Sands

Contact Email: samashi.sands@mail.com

INTRODUCTION

WHAT IS BUDDHISM?

Many individuals nowadays have heard of Buddhism but do not fully comprehend its meaning and practice. When most people think of Buddhism, they envision Buddha sitting with his legs crossed in front of him, his hands on his lap, and his face serene. Many people have been perplexed as to how Buddhism can be called a religion while having no God. Is it possible to practice religion without believing in God? Many people, particularly those from the Western world, find it difficult to understand. Even though Buddhism does not fulfill the ultimate definition of religion, it has attracted millions of people worldwide and many people practice it to this day. According to statistics, Buddhists represent six to seven percent of the world's population.

According to the Pew Research Center, there were around 488 million Buddhists worldwide in 2010. This represented 6% of the world's total population. Between 2010 and 2030, the global Buddhist population is anticipated to grow to 511 million,

However, after 2030, the global Buddhist population is expected to diminish, falling to around 486 million by 2050. The Asia-Pacific area is home to the vast majority of all Buddhists worldwide, accounting for around 95% of all Buddhists worldwide. China has the most Buddhists, accounting for roughly half of all Buddhists. Other nations with considerable Buddhist populations exist outside of China. Thailand has 13%, Japan has 9%, Myanmar (Burma) has 8%, Sri Lanka has 3%, Vietnam has 3%, Cambodia has 3%, South Korea has 2%, India has 2%, and Malaysia has 1%. Other countries have fewer Buddhists since other religions predominate in certain areas. However, in the Western world, North America and Europe have more than one million Buddhists. Each country has 3.9 million and 1.3 million people, respectively.

In recent times, most Buddhist adherents are older than the overall population. This data compares the age of Buddhists to the general population's median age in various locations. The median age is the age at which a group of people is divided into two statistical groups. In a certain region, age influences whether someone is considered young or elderly. In two of the three primary regions where Buddhist data is available: African sub-Saharan Buddhists have a median age of 29 compared to the general population's median age of 18; however, in Asia and the Pacific, Buddhists have a median age of 34 compared to the general population's median age of 29.

ORIGIN

So, where did Buddhism come from exactly? You may inquire. Now you're going to find out.

Buddhism arose in Northern India from a small religious community. It was created by an Indian man named Siddhartha

INTRODUCTION

Guatama. Siddhartha was of aristocratic birth, raised in grandeur and prosperity. This occurred in 566 BC. Like any other nobleman's child, he was well-versed in Indian culture, philosophy, and religious beliefs and customs. He, like the young of his time, was interested not only in obtaining fundamental living necessities such as food, clothing, and shelter but also in discovering the meaning and purpose of life and the key nature of reality.

He then abandoned his luxurious lifestyle and began living a modest life. After many years of suffering, Siddhartha sat under a tree and experienced an 'awakening' to the purpose of existence. This was a watershed point in his life because he realized that "all of life is suffering." He also discovered the road to the end of suffering. From then on, Siddhartha was referred to as Buddha, which means "Awakened One." He began teaching Buddhism and aided others in accepting the life of pain and walking the path to the end of suffering.

When Buddha preached his doctrines, Buddhism spread like wildfire throughout India by word of mouth, as did all Indian religions at the time. It took several generations and 400 years after Buddha's death for it to be written down in Sri Lanka.

Buddhism flourished throughout the world after Buddha's death, from India to Japan, China, Sri Lanka (formerly known as Ceylon), Tibet, Southeast Asia, and the Western world. Because so many people embraced Buddhism, it underwent several significant transformations and became adaptable enough to be adopted by individuals from all walks of life all over the world. Because of the huge changes that have occurred over the years, it has also become difficult to define Buddhism and how one might be educated about it.

INTRODUCTION

As a result, it is acceptable to conclude that Buddhism is the unfolding tale of Buddha and the many generations of followers who have influenced Buddhism in India, Asia, and the rest of the globe in some way. Buddha is credited with all of its teachings, spiritual practices, beliefs, and traditions.

Despite the enormous changes that have occurred in Buddhism over the years, the essential teachings of Buddha have not been lost. He called these lessons "the four noble truths." These noble truths include the existence of suffering ('Dukhka'), 'Trishna', which means that every suffering has a cause, which is either craving or attachment, 'Nirvana', which is the cessation of suffering, and finally, the road to the cessation of suffering. All of them are fundamental teachings that underpin all Buddhist beliefs and practices. They are the foundation of Buddhism. These principles encourage Buddhists to believe in the law of cause and effect, often known as Karma, and the theory of reincarnation, which is a cycle of existence.

Buddhism has been adopted by millions of people all across the world over the years. Followers of Buddhism have earned significant benefits by adhering to the core teachings of Buddhism. If you are thinking of starting Buddhism, perhaps this list of benefits will help you make a decision as quickly as possible.

Buddhism blends well with any religious system. Yes, it makes no difference what religion one follows or what personal belief system one has. Buddhism benefits everyone regardless of their lifestyle or religion. "Believe nothing, no matter where you read it, no matter who said it, no matter if I said it unless it agrees with your reason and common sense," Buddha stated. So it should not disturb you if you are not Indian, Chinese, or Asian; you can embrace Buddhism and reap its benefits.

INTRODUCTION

Meditation provides healing in Buddhism. Meditation was a Hindu technique that Buddha included in his teachings. He promoted and practiced meditation as a means of attaining enlightenment. This tool assists followers in bringing healing into their lives and breaking undesirable habits like smoking and gambling. It also assists Buddhists in healing from previous shortcomings and moving on to bigger things in life. "No matter how difficult your past has been, you can always begin," Buddha stated. Meditation can help you recover and start over.

Buddhism not only heals the past, but it also helps one handle bodily discomfort. A study was conducted on a group of patients with terminal conditions, some of whom were meditators and others who were not. The study found that meditators could endure pain better than non-meditators. Meditators also had a lower sensitivity to pain. Buddhists benefit from this in terms of health and physical tolerance.

It benefits physical health. Buddhism promotes love for oneself and others. Buddhists believe that happiness stems from the inside. As a result, Buddhists are inspired to maintain excellent health standards. From nutrition to exercise and spirituality. Buddhism promotes the consumption of nutritious foods and the avoidance of drugs and other potentially harmful substances. These assist Buddhists in keeping a close eye on their food and physical health. Yoga is a Buddhist technique for keeping the body fit and flexible.

Patience expansion. This is for you if you are easily irritated. Meditation in Buddhism aids in the development of patience. When a person meditates regularly, he or she may become tolerant of someone or something that used to anger them. Meditation teaches people how to manage their brains and focus on

INTRODUCTION

what they are most interested in. It also promotes the attention of others, which aids in the development of understanding for and between individuals.

It promotes generosity. Yes, there is no greater way to serve society than to be generous. In the three central disciplines of Buddhism, Dana, Sila, and Bhavana, or generosity, morality, and meditation, Buddha teaches individuals to be generous. According to Buddha, one should give something as if throwing it away. This applies not only to humans but also to animals and insects. He also encourages us to donate not only something we don't use, but also something we would use. This would demonstrate a far higher level of charity.

It slows down the aging process. Everyone would prefer to age slowly. I'm sure I would. Zen meditation in Buddhism is an excellent tool for this. If you meditate frequently, especially Zen meditation, your breathing rates may be reduced, causing you to take in less oxygen. This aids in the anti-aging process.

Improves self-awareness. Meditation in Buddhism helps people become more aware of themselves. Meditation can help people realize bad parts of their minds, such as self-defeating thoughts and thought habits, among other things. With this understanding, one can better understand themselves, their limitations, strengths, emotional triggers, and many other aspects of themselves. Self-inquiry meditation is an example of such meditation.

As you can see, Buddhism is quite beneficial. But how does one incorporate this way of life or practice in today's world? Most people believe that meditation is rarely a source of enjoyment in today's hectic society. This, however, is not the case because Buddhism is a way of life rather than a religion. Meditation in Buddhism is extremely beneficial for relaxing and relieving tension. It is a strategy that, when utilized correctly, can help one improve in character, mind, and behavior.

In truth, several meditation practices can help you cope with today's hectic lifestyle. Zen meditation, for example, teaches us to slow down in life and focus on obtaining true happiness from within. While others are preoccupied with the day-to-day activities of life, Zen meditators become open to many elements of their lives and improve them via meditation. This meditation approach tests all aspects of life, including profession, health, social life, and spirituality. Talk about a well-balanced life wheel. Who wouldn't want to accomplish that?

1 BUDDHISM PHILOSOPHY

Buddhism, like all religions, is founded on particular ideas, principles, and practices. Buddha gave various teachings on the existence of pain and how to endure and eventually achieve the cessation of suffering. Buddha derived lessons that were extremely beneficial to his followers from these ideas. These teachings addressed several aspects of life and guided how to acquire or practice each of them. These were lessons and teachings that led to a road of awakening and enlightenment. The Three Universal Truths, The Four Noble Truths, The Five Precepts of Buddhism, and The Eightfold Path are examples of such teachings.

These are the core concepts of Buddhism, and each deals with a wide range of teachings and paths of action, as you will see.

THE THREE UNIVERSAL TRUTHS

The Three Universal Truths, also known as The Three Seals, are the fundamental teachings of Buddhism from which all other teachings are derived. These three truths, according to Buddhist teachings, are the qualities of existence. These truths are Annica (all things are impermanent), Dhukka (suffering), and Anatta (achievement of no self). These three teachings form the foundation of Buddhism.

Buddha sat under a tree one day, reflecting on the various aspects of life. He fantasized about the beauty of life and the environment. How lovely the flowers were, and how the sun rays caught the foliage. It was taken aback by him. However, as he continued to meditate, he learned that beneath all the belayed sorrow. Even though life and the environment were wonderful, there was still the presence of misery, and everything appeared to pass. The beauty of the flowers and their blossom would fade with time. He perceived the presence of death in life, as well as the presence of sorrow in all beauty. His eyes were opened to the circle of life, and he became aware of the Three Universal Truths.

ANNICA

The Truth of Impermanence, also known as the Truth of Duration, states that everything in this life endures for a limited duration. It highlights the unavoidable feature of life's transformation. Everything needs to change. For example, as humans, we have a life chronology. We are born, go through puberty, become adults, marry and have children, age, and eventually die. A flower blossoms and then withers over time. Nothing is eternal. Indeed, "Change is the only thing that exists and remains permanent."

As a result, this reality teaches us to accept change. We don't have an option. Life is full of ups and downs. Annica explains why we should learn to let things go and not cling to life's problems. It also provides reassurance in times of adversity, reminding one that periods of suffering are fleeting and will pass. Sadness will eventually give way to joy, and death will give way to life.

Through Annica, Buddha demonstrated that even pain has rewards. For example, a creature's death gives humus to the soil, making it fertile. The deceased body also becomes food for worms, who in turn feed the birds. Nothing is at stake. Everything goes through a life cycle.

DHUKKA

This implies the presence of suffering. The central subject of Buddhism's teachings is suffering. Dhukka highlights the notion that because everything changes and nothing is permanent, life is filled with misery. We suffer not only in this life but also in our next reincarnation and rebirth.

ANATTA

This is the 'No Self' state. Yes, this is the state of the enlightenment sought by Buddhists. It is said that in this state, one is egoless and selfless. It's difficult to believe, yet Anatta is the only place where one can find his or her true self. In the state of immense self, one is completely unselfish, with no selfish tendencies. There is a lack of cravings and longings in Anatta. As a result, we are encouraged to practice selflessness and strive for a life devoid of desire. Anatta warns us to be egoless, to see others as superior, and to have the proper mindset in all situations.

THE FOUR NOBLE TRUTHS

As he continued to meditate, Buddha gained further understanding regarding suffering, which he shared with the populace. "I teach suffering, its origin, cessation, and path," Buddha declared over 2500 years ago. "I only teach that." He learned more about suffering and developed The Four Noble Truths, which form the foundation of Buddhism.

DHUKKA

As stated before in the text, Dhukka is the existence of suffering. We are vulnerable to suffering as humans and species. Nothing is permanent, as you are well aware. Every gain has an equal and opposite cost in our life. As a result, we are subjected to various sorts of unavoidable suffering, including death.

Many may see this as a pessimistic view of life, yet according to Buddha, the presence of suffering in life is unavoidable. "What, monks, is the truth of suffering?" he said. Birth involves agony, as is degradation, sickness, and death. Suffering is being separated from something you enjoy. To want something and not be able to obtain it is to suffer. In short, the human personality, prone to cling and attachment, causes suffering."

No matter how content a person is in life, he or she is prone to suffering in some form. Suffering is caused not only by external circumstances such as the death of a loved one or illness but also by internal factors such as a lack of contentment and fulfillment in life.

The realization of this truth exposes our eyes to the fact that suffering is an unavoidable aspect of life. This truth, especially in these current times, helps us accept the dynamics of life and maintain a positive outlook on life. For example, if a person loses their job, the Dhukka truth can assist them in accepting the change that has occurred in their lives, accepting the new state produced by the shift, and focusing on the new chapter that is about to begin in their lives.

SAMUDAYA

That "suffering has a cause" is the second noble truth. During his meditation, Buddha saw that, because of the impermanence of life, humans create attachments to people and things. When people lose what they are attached to, they develop wants that lead them to suffer. Buddha said it best when he remarked, "Desire brings forth suffering." Buddha also blamed suffering on other factors such as ignorance, anger, or harmful impulses. But how is this possible?

Every day, we as humans have a variety of desires. These aspirations could include, among other things, a desire for success, sensual pleasure, and bodily fulfillment. When these desires and cravings are satisfied, the contentment is typically fleeting, and new desires and cravings take their place. Humans and other creatures are always in pain as a result of this.

When the desire is not restrained, it can lead to increased misery in society. This is evident in current events occurring all around the world, such as addictions, the presence of rogue enterprises, and corrupt governments. The thirst for wealth and power has led many people to commit horrific crimes, causing suffering to others. Gluttony, corruption, and even murders can result from desire.

This reality both enlightens and instructs us to exercise self-control over our wants and to be cautious about what we do. Otherwise, we will be subject to the law of Karma, which holds that "for every event that occurs, there will follow another event whose existence was caused by the first, and this second event will be pleasant or unpleasant depending on whether its cause was skillful or unskillful." This is also known as the law of cause and effect, which states that all acts have repercussions.

As a result, we should be observant of others and maintain a positive attitude in all situations. This allows us to exercise positive aspirations while also living in wisdom and compassion for others.

NIRODHA

The third reality highlights the end of suffering. Yes, sorrow, like everything else, is fleeting. However, to experience this cessation of suffering, one must be prepared to let go of attachments and wants. As Buddha described it, a lack of desires leads to estrangement. Buddha explained that when one reaches this condition of ultimate freedom, "passion fades out." He is released as his enthusiasm fades. When he is liberated, he is aware that he is liberated. 'Birth is exhausted, the holy life has been lived out, what may be done is done, there is no more beyond,' he realizes.

This is referred to as the Buddhist state of Nirvana/Nibbana. All Buddhists strive for this level of enlightenment. In this state, desires such as greed, illusion, and wrath are extinguished. What a wonderful joy it must be to be free of bad feelings and fears.

With this reality, we can be confident that life's sorrows are not permanent, and that we can be released via meditation. This truth, which we encounter every day, compels us to examine our desires and guarantee that we are positive for others. This reality also inspires us to continue through life's journey, keeping our sights fixed on the ultimate goal of emancipation.

MAGGA

Magga asserts as the final noble truth that the Eightfold Path must be followed to achieve freedom from suffering. In this view, Buddha is regarded as a physician, with the Eightfold Path serving as his prescription for enlightenment.

THE EIGHTFOLD PATH

This is easily characterized as the path to enlightenment. According to Buddha, this way reduces human suffering and leads to ultimate freedom. Unlike many spiritual teachings, this path takes on a cheerful and warm tone, informing people on the right thing to do rather than the bad thing to avoid. This affirmative tone facilitates self-empowerment more than prohibitions do.

Panna (Wisdom), Sila (Morality), and Samadhi (Meditation) are the three divisions of the path. This does not, however, imply that each division is independent of the others. All specified rights must be exercised concurrently to be free of suffering.

Among these rights are:

Above all, one must have a correct grasp of the three fundamental facts of existence: Annica (Impermanence of all things), Dhukka (Suffering), Anatta (Achievement of No-self), and the Four Noble Truths. There would be no need for the Eightfold Path if there was no insight.

Buddhists seek teachings and commentaries from Buddhist instructors and practice constant meditation to obtain the proper insight.

Right Thinking - Once clear knowledge has been achieved, it is necessary to practice having the right thinking. A person's thinking influences the direction his or her life will take. Positive thoughts produce a positive character, which results in a positive existence. The same is true when it comes to negative thinking. Buddha emphasized that to practice correct thinking, one must reject worldly pleasures and selfishness, show compassion, and have goodwill toward all people. With these actions, we can live a positive, wise life.

Right Speech - The way we speak reveals a lot about the state of our minds. Positive thoughts are demonstrated by positive verbal speech. To practice proper communication, we must refrain from lying, cursing, gossiping, verbal abuse, hurtful speaking, and swearing. Instead of using negative language, use compassion and sweetness. This will cause you to think positively.

appropriate Action - With good ideas and appropriate speech, your actions will be right as well. This includes abstaining from vices such as stealing, killing, irresponsible sexual behavior, abuse, and molestation, among others. Taking the appropriate activities leads to the proper outcomes in life and fruitfulness.

Right livelihood - Because we are desiring beings, we are prone to participate in corrupt and harmful actions to make ends meet. This should be avoided, and instead, high integrity should be observed in occupations, businesses, and many types of professions. To do this, one should avoid dishonesty, criminality, the human slave trade, drug trafficking, and anything else that could hurt a human or animal.

Right Effort - Anything worthwhile necessitates effort. One should make an effort to observe the correct things in life and never give up on letting go of the negative aspects of their existence. Positive ideas and behaviors should be performed consistently, while negative ones should be avoided.

Being attentive simply means being aware of one's body, emotions, mind, and thoughts. This promotes individuals to be aware of their bodies, emotions, behaviors, and words. With the correct awareness, you may have a clear picture of who you are and keep bad ideas and actions at bay. Meditation is one tool that can aid in this process.

Right Concentration - Our minds frequently wander on a variety of topics, and we find ourselves controlled by our minds. Getting the appropriate concentration means training your mind to focus on what you want. It is having control over your thoughts and focusing your mind on what you want. Constant meditation can help you attain this.

FIVE PRECEPTS OF BUDDHISM

These are the principles that Buddhists follow. In the Christian religion, they are analogous to the Ten Commandments given to Moses. Indeed, the precepts are nearly identical to the second part of the Ten Commandments. Unlike in Christianity, where commandments are viewed as rules, Buddhists view precepts as guidelines or recommendations. Buddhists believe that by following these commandments, they accumulate good karma and go closer to enlightenment.

These are the principles:

- I undertake the precepts to refrain from killing.
- I undertake the precepts to refrain from stealing.
- I undertake the precepts to refrain from any sexual misconduct.
- I undertake the precepts to refrain from incorrect speech or lying.
- I undertake the precepts to refrain from any intoxicants and drugs that can reduce consciousness.

These Buddhist instructions are extremely beneficial to all individuals, Buddhists and non-Buddhists alike. They provide a clear distinction between wrong and right, good and evil, as guides. They also advocate for the right of all living creatures to live. By observing them, one might acquire a soft and compassionate heart toward others.

All choices, good and bad, have consequences. In this day and age, the Buddhist Precepts serve as moral checkpoints and aid in the avoidance of self-destructive behavior. This promotes self-control, which is essential for personal development. This also protects against calamities such as sexually transmitted diseases, drug and sex addiction, and violence, all of which are the result of poor decisions.

The Five Precepts foster harmonious cohabitation in society on the social platform. Morality cautions people's behavior and the consequences of our activities on society. Adherence to high moral standards, as a result, increases the level of integrity and peaceful living among members of a community. With morality, vices such as murder, corruption, theft, and many others are greatly reduced, creating a favorable climate for social growth and development.

Observing the noble precepts leads to spiritual growth. When you follow the precepts, you are assured an abundance of wisdom, peace in your life despite your suffering, and eventually true enlightenment beyond death.

2 SCHOOLS OF BUDDHISM

Over time, people all across the world have embraced and practiced religion. However, because of diversity, the religions practiced have various branches within them. More akin to sects. Shiite and Sunni Muslims, for example, exist alongside Catholics and Evangelicals among Christians.

Buddhism, like any other religion, is divided into sects. These cults offer various techniques that are all beneficial in their way. These are referred to as Buddhist Schools. They have passed down Buddhist views and practices through centuries, and while some teachings and practices alter, the fundamental concepts have stayed constant. The two great schools of Buddhism are Theravada and Mahayana. These branches of Buddhism are taught and practiced in various places of the world.

THERAVADA BUDDHISM (SCHOOL OF THE ELDERS)

Theravada Buddhism, also known as Mantrayana, is the most conservative of the schools. They are quite traditional and monastic and take the Pali (Buddha texts) very seriously. They have a strong belief in the existence of pain and impermanence. Because nothing is permanent, Theravada Buddhists believe that there is nothing in the world to desire or cling to. They think that one should strive for mental and spiritual purity regularly. As a result, they place an emphasize individual enlightenment through meditation, pursuing wisdom, and living a virtuous life.

Following the principles and the Eightfold Path of Buddhism to the letter, according to Theravada Buddhists, leads to the ultimate gift of Nirvana. According to all Buddhists, Nirvana is obtaining enlightenment and escaping from the cycle of rebirth and death.

Theravada Buddhism is mostly taught in Southeast Asian countries such as Sri Lanka, Laos, Thailand, Cambodia, and Burma.

MAHAYANA BUDDHISM (THE GREAT VEHICLE)

Northern Asia is where Mahayana Buddhism is taught. It is found in China, Korea, Tibet, Japan, and, later, areas of India. While Theravada Buddhists adhere to Pali principles, Mahayana Buddhists adhere to Tibetan and Chinese canons. These canons are quite similar to Buddha's original teachings, but they include additional texts and commentaries that are solely for the Mahayana.

In contrast to Theravada, the Mahayana school focuses on enlightening not only oneself but also others. They concentrate on developing a Bodhisattva mentality. Bodhisattva is a Sanskrit word that means "enlightened one." Their teachings primarily emphasize compassion for all sentient species and wisdom. Mahayana Buddhists believe that one should look not only at the inner but also at the exterior.

The Mahayana Buddhists believe that the enlightened ones, Bodhisattva, postpone their Nirvana so that they can continue to serve others who are striving for enlightenment. The Mahayana also promotes constant meditation to obtain what they refer to as "skillful means" that assist them in dealing with emotional and mental concerns, allowing them to guide and counsel others toward enlightenment.

Mahayana Buddhism is commonly regarded as an umbrella term that encompasses various varieties of Buddhism such as Zen Buddhism and a portion of Tibetan Buddhism.

ZEN BUDDHISM

Zen is a Japanese pronunciation of the Chinese term Ch'an, which means meditation. It combines Mahayana, Indian Buddhism, and Taoism.

Zen is supposed to have been founded by an Indian guru named Bodhidharma. It is reported that he brought Zen teachings from India to China. After a few years, it was introduced to Japan in the 13th century, where it was practiced until it spread to other Western nations in the 20th century.

The teachings of Bodhidharma primarily emphasize meditation as a means of reaching ultimate freedom. He preached that all humans have already attained enlightenment, but that ignorance has obscured their ability to do so.

To achieve this enlightenment, Zen teachings place a greater focus on meditation than on text study, religious ritual practice, and ideology adherence.

Though Zen Buddhists place less emphasis on scripture, they have produced their texts over the years. These works combine core Buddhist teachings with borrowed ideas and writing styles such as Taoism, Chinese poetry and folk sayings, and Confucius's wisdom. These characteristics make Zen literature appealing to Americans and Europeans. Zen Buddhism also promotes artistic endeavors such as painting, calligraphy, and archery.

Zen Buddhists follow a tradition known as Zazen, which translates as "sitting Zen." This meditation is performed while seated, hence the name. It is simple and easy to accomplish because all one has to do is sit, relax, and focus on breathing in his or her stomach. While meditating, one should strive for absolute attention and a deep sensation of being present. Zazen is practiced differently by different Zen Buddhists. As a result, there are two distinct forms of Zen Buddhism: Soto Zen and Rinzai Zen. Soto Zen emphasizes silent meditation with an empty mind of all thoughts and philosophies. Rinzai Zen, on the other hand, is known for meditating using the Koan, which is a riddle or worded question presented to a practitioner by his or her teacher. The practitioner is supposed to examine the koan until its actual meaning becomes clear. The practitioner is then expected to share the revelation with his or her teacher to determine whether or not the revelation is correct and to get advice.

Though Zen meditation can be practiced alone, it is advised that one work with a Zen teacher for direction and in-depth exploration of the Zen practice.

TIBETAN BUDDHISM

Tibetan Buddhism is a Mahayana Buddhist sect from Tibet. Its rituals and beliefs extended to regions surrounding the Himalayas like Mongolia, Nepal, and Bhutan over time. It also has adherents in northern China, Russia, and India.

Its teachings combine core Buddhist teachings with Tibetan traditions. Some have referred to it as Vajrayana Buddhism since it shares characteristics with Vajrayana Buddhist teachings that have been preserved in Tibet. Vajrayana Buddhism is quite similar to Mahayana Buddhism, with only minor distinctions. Whereas Mahayana teachings advocate putting wants, ignorance, and enmity to death, Vajrayana teachings advocate turning all of that into wisdom. In contrast to Mahayana Buddhism, Vajrayana Buddhism values the student-teacher relationship. According to Tibetan traditions, a lama (teacher) is particularly important on the path to enlightenment.

Tibetan Buddhism integrates yoga practices and tantras, which are the visualization of meditational deities, in addition to meditation. They also use mudras, which are ritual hand movements, mandalas, which are emblems of the enlightened world, and mantras, which are sacred symbols and phrases.

The three vehicles of Buddhism are traditionally emphasized in Tibetan teachings. These three vehicles concentrate on Buddha's fundamental teachings. They are the 'Hinayana' (the narrow vehicle), which consists of Buddha's original teachings and practices, the 'Mahayana' (greater vehicle), which focuses on achieving compassion towards living beings for the benefit of others, and the Vajrayana (indestructible vehicle), which focuses on having a guru to empower them on the path of spiritual development and enlightenment.

Tibetan Buddhism is divided into four schools: Nyingma, Kagyu, Sakya, and Geluk. While each school has a unique history, its teachings all trace back to the original Buddha teachings.

Nyingma means "ancient" in Tibetan. Padmasambhava's disciples founded this school. The term remained true to its meaning because the 'Nyingma' lineage was the first true Tibetan Buddhist school. Padmasambhava's main pupils, including a woman named Yeshe Tsogyal, created the 'Nyingma' lineage in Tibet. The Vajrayana teachings of the earlier royal period were followed by the Nyingma School.

The Kagyu, Sakya, and Geluk schools, on the other hand, adhered to the subsequent Vajrayana doctrines brought to Tibet from India. Each school was founded by a single guru who formed lineages and taught several enigmatic ideologies. These schools still exist today.

While Zen and Tibetan Buddhism are both Mahayana Buddhist traditions, they differ in their teachings and practices. Zen Buddhists, for example, are concerned with the nature of one's mind, whereas Tibetan Buddhists seek spiritual growth.

Meditation is emphasized as the way to enlightenment in Zen Buddhism teachings. Its adherents believe that meditation provides numerous perspectives on life and our existence, resulting in enlightenment. Tibetan Buddhism, on the other hand, emphasizes attaining Buddhahood for the sake of others. They participate in activities that benefit others.

While Zen Buddhists are open to reading scripture, doing rituals, and worshiping a deity, Tibetan Buddhists believe that one's deeds are critical in achieving enlightenment. According to Tibetan teachings, to achieve ultimate happiness, one should rid oneself of worldly wants.

Despite their differences, Zen and Tibetan Buddhism are both extremely beneficial in everyday life. Especially in today's technological society. Many people in today's world are caught up in life's drama and expectations, causing them to live in despair every day. Many people have suffered from depression, and others have attempted suicide. This need not be the case for you or anyone else. The Zen practice of meditation provides an excellent foundation for unwinding from this hectic lifestyle. It not only provides insights into various aspects of life, but it also relieves one of life's many worries and obligations.

There is joy in assisting others. "When you're down, look for someone to help," it's been said. After you have assisted someone, the sadness or tension will fade. As life becomes more hectic by the day, Tibetan Buddhism serves as a helpful reminder that one's activities should be for the benefit of others. This, in turn, aids one's efforts to serve others and support people around him or her. It also serves to keep our morality in check, resulting in great integrity. What a wonderful world it would be to live in an incorruptible society full of upright people - absolute happiness.

The twenty-first century is brimming with many types of enjoyable hobbies and drugs. Among the many examples are drugs, alcohol, sexual misconduct, and violence. It is really easy to adopt hazardous habits. However, by adhering to Tibetan Buddhism, which encourages us to be attentive to ourselves and refrain from worldly pleasure to achieve Buddhahood, one can be relatively certain of personal growth and a healthy life devoid of the effects of a reckless life. Zen Buddhism is concerned with the nature of the mind. As a result, Zen Buddhism uses meditation to help people recognize their limitations, flaws, and harmful habits. Constant Zen meditation could also help you break free from these vices.

We cannot dominate the world by ourselves. With everything that is going on in the world, we are all prone to making bad decisions and taking incorrect turns in life. As a result, we require mentors to advise us in all aspects of our lives. This is highlighted by Tibetan Buddhism, which emphasizes the importance of having a guru or lama in one's life. Following Tibetan Buddhism would arouse in us the need to find a person or two to mentor us in various aspects of life.

Buddhist philosophies have been practiced for centuries. It has spread beyond its Asian roots, with millions of devotees worldwide. Many people have accepted it regardless of color, age, profession, origin, or deity and realized the benefits of becoming a Buddhist disciple. Though times have changed, the fundamental precepts of Buddhism have not.

3 GUIDED BUDDHISM MEDITATION

Buddhists practice meditation to train their minds. Fitness is more commonly used by athletes to train their bodies. Meditation, when done regularly, allows someone to tap into their mental powers and get insight into life's issues. It's also an excellent tool for unwinding. Meditation, according to meditators, is healthy for the mind and soul.

It would be difficult for a beginner to sit for hours on end in meditation. Meditation necessitates practice. As a result, there are guided Buddhist meditation practices that teach the fundamentals of Buddhist meditation. distinct strategies concentrate on distinct mental abilities. It is therefore advisable to seek out a meditation master to provide direction through meditation.

Among the most well-known strategies are:

WALKING MEDITATION

Walking meditation is another name for mindful walking. It is one of the most prevalent meditation activities. What exactly is the point? Is it about paying attention to your steps while you walk? That is a large part of it, but walking meditation is more than just walking. It affects more than just the physical component of the body.

For thousands of years, there have been several styles of meditation known as movement meditations. Walking Meditation has been the most widely practiced of all the forms. When you think about it, it is the most practical of all.

For beginners, mindful walking is ideal. When trying out seated meditations, persons who are always on the go, busy, or restless are highly suggested. This is not to say that seated meditations are not possible. It's only that as a beginning, you'll see results quickly from walking meditation. After a week or so, one can begin seated meditations and practice frequently. You can practice a combination of sitting and walking meditations at different times. Walking meditation is ideal for times when you are pressed for time.

Find a suitable place to meditate now. Mostly, a location where you could walk back and forth. It should be a reasonably calm, secluded, and disturbance-free environment. Walking meditation would undoubtedly appear unusual if practiced in public. You can choose to do it outside or inside. You're good to proceed as long as you're comfortable and have enough space to trace your steps.

Begin your steps now. Take 10-15 steps around the area you've chosen, then halt and breathe for a set amount of time. After a few moments of breathing, turn and go back to where you came from, stopping to breathe once more. When you've finished breathing, turn around and continue walking.

Walking meditation entails intentionally noticing a set of behaviors that come naturally to you. Noting these stages as you go may feel strange, even ludicrous, but don't let that distract you. Try to remember the fundamental elements of each step as you walk. These aspects include lifting the foot off the ground, forward movement of the foot, placing the foot back on the ground (heel first), shifting body weight to the forward leg, and lifting the back heel while the toes remain on the ground. This cycle will continue.

Observe how your rear foot swings forward and hits the ground as you lift it entirely off the ground. Watch it as it makes heel-first contact with the ground; feel the weight shift back onto that foot as the body travels forward.

Walking meditation does not require speed, however, many practitioners suggest short, leisurely steps. Do not exaggerate or alter the steps in any way. Make them look as natural as possible.

Now it's time to work on your hands and arms. You can wear them behind your back, in front, or just dangle loosely at your side. Whichever manner feels most natural to you.

Pay attention to distinct feelings while you walk. Perhaps one or two that you would ordinarily expect. This feeling includes your breathing, the movement of your feet and legs, their contact with the ground or floor, sounds created by your movement, and those made by the environment. Everything that might be of interest to you.

Of course, being human causes your thoughts to wander. Your mind will, without a sure, wander no matter how hard you attempt to focus on the feelings. But don't worry, it's very normal. Don't feel like you've failed if your mind wanders. Simply return your attention to the sensation. Allow your attention to float on the thoughts like a balloon on a wall before returning your attention to the meditation.

So, how can you work walking meditation into your everyday routine? Life is extremely hectic. Many people consider slow, official walking meditation to be a luxury. Nonetheless, the more you practice, the more likely you are to accept it. Even if you only practice for a few minutes. Also, keep in mind that you can walk mindfully at any speed you want. You can even run with time. Of course, your pace and breathing will change, but you can still run. In reality, over time, you may bring the same level of awareness to ordinary life and feel a presence at every moment. It can be a highly effective method for incorporating mindfulness into your daily life.

following consistent practice, you will understand the benefits of kinhin (walking meditation in Japanese), which Zen meditators would perform following sitting meditation sessions of Zazen. You must bring the state that you generally achieve during sitting meditation sessions into the flow of your daily activities.

MINDFULNESS MEDITATION

This meditation focuses on increasing self-consciousness and awareness of one's surroundings. It aids in becoming aware of what is going on in one's body and mind. It heightens awareness of particular bodily sensations and assists the meditator in focusing on specific regions of tension. When practicing mindfulness meditation, the meditator must concentrate on his or her breathing, relax, and be aware of his or her wandering thoughts. It is also necessary not to be concerned with or criticize the thoughts that arise in one's head, but merely to be aware of them. The absence of judgment is critical. Mindfulness meditation helps people become more aware of their mental habits and the consequences of particular mental triggers on their emotions and bodies over time.

The most important aspects to consider when practicing mindfulness techniques are posture, thinking, and breathing, which serve as the anchor- the subject of meditation. Throughout the meditation, the anchor serves as a focal point.

To help you relax, here is a 10-minute mindfulness meditation approach. You have the option of doing this alone or in a group. You have an option. Before you begin, locate a timer or a bell to assist you in timing the meditation session. Once that is completed, take your seat. It might be a pillow, a chair, a bench, or anything else you want to utilize as a seat. Stretch your legs and place your feet flat on the ground once you've settled into your seat. You have the option of keeping your eyes open or closed. Tilt your head slightly and keep your torso straight but not stiff. Rest your hands on your thighs and relax your shoulders. Take some time to feel that posture with your upper arms parallel to your torso.

Now, with your posture correct, concentrate on your breathing. This is your focal point of focus. One may select any anchor of their choice. However, due to its consistency, breath is most suited for this meditation.

To begin, take three conscious breaths. Be entirely aware of each breath as it enters and exits your body. Get in touch with your breathing. Inhale and exhale, inhale and exhale, inhale and exhale.

Pay attention to everything about your breathing to make it more engaging. Concentrate on the rising and falling of your tummy and abdomen. Feel your breath enter and exit your nostrils. Concentrate on your breathing in every detail.

Before long, it is evident that all kinds of thoughts are constantly flooding your mind. It is difficult to focus solely on breathing. The trail of thoughts is uncontrollable, like a flood. There are numerous ideas. These thoughts continue to elicit emotions and experiences in your body. Now, don't dismiss the thoughts. Take note of the thought and return your attention to your breathing in this meditation. As though a small brush stroke on the concept. Touching the notion is regarded as a moment of direct consciousness. Take a quick note of the concept, then return your attention to your breathing. Some thoughts will elicit a wide range of feelings; simply brush your mind across them, focus on your breath, and relax. This makes you more aware of your thoughts and aids in the development of focus.

When you use this approach frequently, you will improve your capacity to manage your mind and choose which thoughts to focus on and which to ignore.

Mindfulness meditation improves someone's mental and physical well-being by eliminating unpleasant feelings that they may have harbored. Mindfulness assists people in becoming more aware of their emotions and triggers. For example, someone living with anxiety may discover the causes of anxiety and how the body reacts to them. Then, via meditation, they will learn to manage their minds and brush away the thoughts that cause anxiety. This helps to reduce anxiety. It can be an excellent technique for reducing hasty emotional reactions such as anger and combating mental illnesses such as melancholy and anxiety.

Mindfulness meditation enhances memory as well. Meditation has been demonstrated by some researchers to affect the left hippocampus, which is the portion of the brain that controls cognitive processes such as memory. Practicing mindfulness meditation techniques improves your memory significantly.

Mindfulness meditation is suggested socially since it assists with relationship pleasure. Mindfulness meditation, with consistent practice, helps one establish equilibrium within themselves while also being aware of their environment. Being aware of one's senses and emotions allows one to cultivate a self-control and understanding attitude toward others. This, in turn, promotes a positive attitude toward others and peace, even under difficult circumstances.

Mindfulness meditation has several health benefits. It is supposed to reduce blood pressure, for example. It certainly does. It is common knowledge that mental stress has a bad impact on our bodies, causing weariness, physical aches, and high blood pressure. It is, in fact, one of the leading causes of high blood pressure. Because mindfulness meditation helps people deal with unpleasant emotions and reduces stress, it has a positive impact on our bodies by promoting relaxation and lowering the negative impacts of stress, such as blood pressure.

When you begin to practice being attentive regularly, you will notice that opportunities to do so will appear almost wherever you look. Here are a few ideas for finding mindfulness when you least expect it.

Find awareness in your daily tasks: While most people consider domestic tasks to be the pinnacle of daily drudgery, adjusting your perspective will present you with an additional opportunity to practice mindfulness. When doing these chores, concentrate on the present moment, calm your mind beforehand, and pay attention to how your hands feel while accomplishing the work.

Consider the sights, sounds, and smells, and after you're done, take a time to enjoy your labor and how much better things are now that it's accomplished.

In the shower, practice mindfulness: Showering is another aspect of the day that many people rush through when, in actuality, it is an excellent opportunity to practice mindfulness. In the shower, all of your senses are always experiencing multiple things at once; take advantage of this by being present and in the moment.

While exercising, keep the following in mind: While it may appear counter-intuitive, the average person's thinking when exercising is very similar to that of someone practicing mindful meditation. This is an excellent moment to concentrate on the movement of your particular body parts and how they feel as they approach their limitations. Consider the sounds, sights, and fragrances as you exercise and concentrate on the present now rather than getting lost in another world while listening to music. Furthermore, running mindfully has been demonstrated to improve performance and endurance.

Practice being attentive while using social media: Although it may appear counterintuitive, if you make a concerted effort, you can even practice mindfulness meditation while using any sort of social media. While the siren's song of a social media notification might easily pull you out of the moment during various types of mindfulness meditation, if you set aside time to check in on what your friends are up to, you can achieve a level of awareness while doing so.

To make this sort of mindfulness meditation work, the first thing you need to do is eliminate any other potential distractions before you begin. This is a very important step because the majority of individuals use social networking sites to multitask. After you've cleared your mind of any distractions, you'll want to attempt to enter the present as much as possible. With the correct mindset in place, you can then examine the images or words relating to your history to fully inhabit those prior events.

Consider what was going on at the time of the creation for every image you see or tweet you read. Remember how you felt at the time and let the recollection wash over you. Attempt to put yourself in the moment and place in question by recalling the numerous messages your body was sending you at the time.

KUNDALINI YOGA

Transcendental meditation is a technique for reducing worry and increasing energy. The term "Kundalini" refers to the richness of energy found near the base of the spine. Kundalini yoga focuses on the energy and helps it awaken, resulting in happiness, self-awareness, and health. Yogi Bhajan, an Indian government employee, popularized Kundalini in 1968. He popularized Kundalini Yoga in North America, particularly in Toronto and Los Angeles.

A Kundalini yoga class incorporates asana (postures), meditation, and chanting. Teachers who have been trained in the Kundalini tradition wear white and mainly play the gong in class. A Kundalini Yoga practice is commonly referred to as a Yogi.

Two energy lines move up and around the base of the spine. These lines cross seven well-known places known as chakras. Each chakra serves a distinct purpose in our body, keeping us healthy. Kundalini postures are distinguished by rhythmic and steady motions that initiate the flow of energy and correct any imbalances in the chakras. When the energy flows, the yogi becomes more in tune with reality and enters a higher state of consciousness. This increase in self-awareness and peace leads to a more productive and happy life.

WHAT EXACTLY ARE CHAKRAS?

Understanding chakras requires an understanding of energy. Everything is made up of energy, which is continually in motion as it flows and transforms from one form to another. The chakras are essentially groups of energy that have been given names to help you comprehend what you're working with. This is a pretty basic description, but we will start delving into the intricacies of these energies and how to control them (and how they affect you!)

You've almost certainly come across the word chakra at some point in your life. You might have noticed a friend wearing an unusual bracelet with bright stones, heard references while learning how to meditate, or met an instructor in a guided yoga session. But who are these enigmatic beings, what do they do, and where do they originate from? Chakras are thought to be circular spinning wheels that emit spiritual energy and are a reference to the source of spiritual illumination within the body. The name chakra translates to "wheel" in its native Sanskrit. From the tail bone to the top of the head, these energy centers correspond with the spine. Each chakra corresponds to important bodily, mental, and spiritual processes. Maintaining chakra balance is a fantastic method to become more in tune with yourself and the people around you.

In this book, we will concentrate on seven chakras. Although there are up to a hundred and fourteen chakras throughout the body, these are the most well-known and often discussed! comprehending the fundamental seven throughout your spine will get you a lot closer to comprehending your chakras, spirit, and consciousness.

Let's talk about light for a minute. If you split pure light energy into distinct frequencies, you would observe the light split into the spectrum of the rainbow's seven colors. As you may have guessed, each of the seven chakras corresponds to one of the seven colors of the rainbow. Starting at the base of the spine, there is the red chakra, followed by the orange, yellow, green, blue, indigo, and violet chakras in that order as you progress up the spine. As we progress, we will delve further into each of these chakras and the functions they provide for your physical being as well as your consciousness.

Light is viewed as a wavelength that oscillates or vibrates between two extremes before entering your vision and being interpreted by the brain. This wavelength can be interpreted scientifically as a sine wave. Which color you perceive is determined by the frequency or the relative distance between each oscillation. Likewise, each of your chakras will have its frequency. Red has the longest wavelength, hence it vibrates at the slowest rate. As you move up the rainbow's colors, the oscillations increase, resulting in stronger vibrations, with violet being the quickest.

As the chakras spin, they create a vacuum that draws in all sorts of things from your surroundings. These things can range from sound, light, the earth's magnetic field, microwaves, and even the emotions of those around you. You will feel better and live a healthier life if your chakras are in harmony. Chakras that have decreased their vibration or are vibrating at an excessive rate can lead the chakras around them to get out of sync via a feedback loop or chain reaction. This interruption in the flow of energy can eventually show as irritability in one's mental state, emotional state, or even physical problems. Einstein, one of the greatest philosophers of all time, described nature as neither wholly material nor entirely spiritual. Whether or not this is agreed upon as a philosophy, it will function well as a good metaphor to describe chakras.

So we now have a basic idea of what chakras are, but where did this information come from? The first evidence of chakras comes from India, between 1500 and 500 BC. They are drawn from the Vedas, which are regarded as the earliest records of literary Sanskrit and the ancient Hindu scriptures. An essential difference to emphasize here is that the chakras are not a religious symbol associated with any particular religious practice. They are prominent in both Hinduism and Tantric Buddhism, from which the yogic teachings are derived. The major goal of these teachings is to unite human and heavenly spirits. The fascinating thing about written language is that once it is recorded, it becomes static--a time capsule of the words that were iterated to make sense at that exact point in time. Language and word meanings, as we all know, do not share this unchanging nature. The meaning of words can vary dramatically over the span of a century or even a decade. The colors we see, however, and the frequencies emitted by those light energy, do not alter. The colors of the light spectrum are the same as they were back then.

THE ROOT CHAKRA MULADHARA

Let's start with the root chakra, Muladhara, which is located at the base of the spine at the bottom of the tailbone on the pelvic floor. The root chakra resembles a lotus flower with four petals that bloom outward, each bearing a distinct Sanskrit letter (va, scha, shs, sa) with the word lam inscribed in the center. Its frequency corresponds to the color red, and it is also usually connected with the earth element, the force that keeps us alive. Muladhara is made up of two Sanskrit words: "Mula" (root) and "Dhara" (support). Muladhara serves as the basis for all other chakras in the body, therefore finding balance within it is critical. When the root chakra is out of balance, it is nearly impossible to achieve harmony iwiththe other chakras. If you want to start repairing your chakras and bringing them back into balance, the root chakra is unquestionably the best place to start.

The root chakra corresponds to the organs responsible for elimination and excretion. The colon, bladder, rectum, and kidneys are all included. The bottom of the foot and the sciatic nerve are also crucial regarding the root chakra, as we will see momentarily. The root chakra is also linked to the adrenal glands, which are placed on top of each kidney. This is an important distinction to make since the adrenal glands create the hormone adrenaline, which is responsible for your fight-or-flight response. Because fight or flight is used to safeguard your survival, you can see how the two are related. In addition, the kidneys' function is to filter blood. This, together with the position near the perineum, demonstrates the link to excretion on multiple levels. The root chakra energy's principal function is to aid with survival. Competitiveness, safety, fear, and security are also attributes influenced by the root chakra. Furthermore, it is intended to connect you to the earth to ground you. Consider the root chakra to be the roots of a tree, connecting the spirit to the earth's soils. The root chakra illuminates your most natural desires and serves as an energy source for acquiring food, and shelter and empowering your sexual drive. The root chakra, more than any other chakra, is linked to your physical vitality. Finally, on an emotional level, the root chakra influences the most basic emotions: anger, happiness, and sadness.

When Muladhara becomes overactive, it manifests as fear, panic, and worry. You may feel anxious and restless in its modest form. If the overactivity is serious enough, the person may experience anxiety or even paranoia. We've already discussed how the fight or flight reaction is linked to Muladhara. Fear is a vital emotion that exists to protect the body from danger. An overactive root chakra can send dread and worry into the body even when there is no impending threat. If you have PTSD, generalized anxiety, hypochondria, or obsessive-compulsive disorder, you should consider working on balancing the first chakra. These illnesses are strongly linked to fear and the fight or flight response, and hence to the root chakra. If you are overactive for an extended period, you may begin to experience the physical symptoms of an out-of-balance root chakra. Digestive disorders, lower back or hip pain, and ovarian or prostate problems can all occur. When Muladhara is not active or is obstructed, you may feel an entirely distinct set of symptoms. Because survival needs have been generally met for a long period, the root chakra becomes less active in an imbalanced fashion. While this may not appear to be the worst difficulty to have, it is still critical to achieving a sense of balance and togetherness. Daydreaming, lack of concentration, being spacey, or having "your head in the clouds" can all be symptoms of underactive root chakras. To put it another way, there isn't much to cause adrenaline or a fight or flight response. Muladhara's equilibrium will bring you calm, confidence, and vitality. When thinking about money, physical safety, and shelter, someone with a balanced root chakra will not feel anxious or aloof. Rather, those thoughts will be welcomed with calm mindfulness and appreciation.

So, now that we know what the root chakra is and some of the key roles it serves, let us look at how to get it into balance and how to keep it there once it is. Have you heard the term "earthing" before? The most typical method of earthing is to go barefoot in an outside area. Consider this: if your daily routine is typical, you presumably wear shoes for the majority of the day and walk on surfaces that isolate us from the planet. Carpet, tile, or linoleum is separated twice by the building's foundation as well as the rubber soles of your shoes. Have you ever noticed a significant increase in your personal energy levels after strolling barefoot on the sands of a beach or through the soils of a woody forest? The surface of the planet emits energy, just as the human body and the surface of the sun do. When we are isolated from this energy, we can get tired and angry.

Every environment contains naturally occurring particles with a positive or negative charge. The word negative here refers to the particle's charge rather than the consequences of the particle on the human body. Positive ions can be damaging to the human body, whereas negative ions might be beneficial. Positive ions are electron-deficient particles that have fewer electrons than protons. Negative ions are the inverse of positive ions, with more electrons than protons. The earth's energy comprises a high concentration of negatively charged ions. Negative ions can also be found in large numbers in the natural, clean air found around waterfalls, the ocean, and highly forested places. The concentration is considerably higher now that positive ions have been cleaned by a recent storm.

The soles of the feet are porous, with a dense network of sebaceous glands. These glands serve as an exit in the form of sweat, but they also serve as an entry point for the negatively charged energy that comes from the soil. When energy enters the body, Sudomotor neurons transport negative ions up the sciatic nerve, the longest nerve in the human body. The sciatic nerve joins at the base of the spine near the sacrum and, you guessed it, the root chakra Muladhara as it travels up the legs.

While in the air, negative ions bond to bacteria, viruses, mold spores, and other contaminants, rendering them too heavy to remain afloat. A good approach to think about this procedure is to imagine using soap on hands that are too unclean to clean with just water. When soap is lathered on the hands, the charges of the particles within the soap capture the dirt particles, bond to them, and then wash away easily when met with water. Nature's soap is negative ions. What function do negative ions perform once they enter the body? They cleanse and purify the blood, reviving cell metabolism and enhancing the human body's natural immunological function. This can aid to enhance digestion and healthy, deep sleep, both of which have been linked to the root chakra. Positively charged ions, on the other hand, are concentrated in dirty cities, office buildings with computer monitors, intensive air conditioning, and densely populated areas such as schools.

So, we know the benefits of earthing, but sticking our hands in the dirt isn't always the most practical thing to do every day. Perhaps your job needs a lot of plane travel or an hour commute each way before even starting the work day. There are various methods for transmitting negative ions within your home. Himalayan salt is rich in trace elements and can be used to make lamps, candles, and other household goods that emit negative ions. A waterfall will also help you create your negative ions. Though it is not a natural waterfall formation, the disruption of water molecules will shift electrons from the water molecules, releasing negative ions into your home's air. There are also a variety of items available, ranging from bracelets to full-fledged electrical transmitters, with the express objective of producing negative ions while repelling positively charged ones.

When it comes to foods that promote the root chakra, it may come as no surprise that root vegetables such as beets, carrots, onion, garlic, radishes, and parsnips boost root chakra vitality. Protein-rich foods such as meat, beans, tofu, eggs, and nuts also aid to support the root chakra. Finally, eating foods that resonate at the same frequency as the chakra it relates to is a powerful method for balancing any of the 7 chakras. Consider red foods such as apples, raspberries, pomegranates, and tomatoes. Positive affirmations can help balance all of the chakras, not just the root chakra. If you haven't tried this technique yet, you might be amazed at the impact that merely telling oneself nice things can have on living a healthy and happy life. Positive affirmations that will help balance the root chakra include the following:

- "I'm safe and secure right where I am."
- "I have a healthy mind, body, and spirit."
- "I deserve to have the help I need whenever I need it."
- "I will live an abundant life with those who care for me and those who care for me."
- "Right now, I am grounded and relaxed."

Kayakalpa is an ancient medical science that deals with spiritual liberation and longevity. Some say the practices date back over a thousand years! By looking at the Sanskrit words that make up the term, we may gain a sense of what Kayakalpa entails. Kaya is the word for body, while Kalpa is the word for metamorphosis. These teachings are derived from the Vedic writings discussed in the first chapter. The goal is to reverse the effects of aging by using a specific set of therapies to balance the rate of healthy new cell formation with the rate of cell degradation in older tissues. As a result, the aging process is halted. While the concept appears simple once articulated, the actual method of reaching this level of rejuvenation is unique and laborious. Kayakalpa is traditionally regarded to be exclusively attainable to persons of great fortune. The secrets contained in Kayakalpa practices were guarded by the Siddhas, individuals who had attained enlightenment. These methods were mostly available to royalty. Detoxification of the body is accomplished through purgative treatments such as massages, leeches, mineral baths, and oils. After the body has been cleansed of these pollutants, a very nourishing herbal and pharmaceutical cure is administered. Rasyanas are anti-aging herbal medicines that are part of Ayurvedic medical traditions. These processes could frequently take place over several months in a gloomy tent. The fundamental concept is to reverse the metabolic rate of activity in the body's cells. You can see from this basic understanding how wealthy one needs to be in terms of both time and finances to achieve anything like this. Would you be able to take three months off work right now to devote yourself to the yogic practice of Kayakalpa? Not many of us would be able to, but those that could prioritize the purification of the body and mind.

It is critical to discuss the root chakra's role as the entry point for awakening the dormant Kundalini energy in the human spirit. Kundalini energy was incorporated into Hatha yoga teachings around the eleventh century. It is the divine force that, via various tantric practices, can lead to spiritual freedom and joy. Kundalini is a Sanskrit adjective that means "circular" in English. It can also refer to the noun for the word snake and be called "coiled". Physical representations of the Kundalini are frequently associated with images of snakes. Until aroused, the dormant energy is like a coiled snake at the base of the spine. It is one of the components of the "subtle body." The subtle body is made up of nadis, which are energy conduits, prana, which is subtle energy itself, bindu, which are essence drops, and, of course, chakras, which are the subject of this book.

When the Kundalini awakens, it will rise from the Muladhara chakra and go along the side of the spine to the top of the head, where it will find the crown chakra. As the Kundalini energy runs through the spinal pathways, a progressively strong set of ineffable heavenly knowledge and insight becomes visible to the yogi's mental eye as the energy rises through each of the seven chakras. All of the chakras open and align to their full potential and splendor. There are distinct bodily sensations reported during the procedure, such as an electrical current tingling up the spine, a cool breeze felt on the fingertips, and bliss unrelated to any other experience. When this is completed, a dramatic shift in consciousness happens. Some regard it to be the pinnacle of spiritual enlightenment. That is an incredible amount of power stored in your Muladhara chakra!

There are various methods for waking the Kundalini. Some are more passive, while others are more direct and deliberate. It is said that Kundalini awakening can occur whether the yogi is prepared or not. To awaken this strong spiritual force, different disciplines such as pranayama, bandhas, mantra recitation, mudra use, and tantric ritual are performed. The practice of being passively awoken by shaktipat entails transmission by a Guru, teacher, or master who has already undergone the experience. Shaktipat may only temporarily raise the Kundalini, but the student will have a reference point to use as a base for future spiritual enlightenment techniques. A person who has attained Kundalini spiritual enlightenment gets more disconnected from material things while also becoming more compassionate and tolerant. The ego becomes far less involved, and this experience is sometimes referred to as the crucification of the human ego.

Some yogis and ancient literature believe that the vital energy force (prana) spreads throughout the macrocosm and microcosm. In these beliefs, the macrocosm is the entire universe, while the microcosm is the human body. If there are terrestrial creatures on other worlds in the universe, it is due to the presence of prana. Our brains are only supposed to be alive because of Prana's tremendous vitality.

We have effectively addressed a variety of issues about Muladhara, one of the most significant chakras in the entire body. We shall return to this chakra as the book progresses; it is impossible not to because it is intertwined with each individual's overall spiritual well-being. There is more to learn later in this book and from other teachers around the world. Hinduism and Tantric Buddhism have profound ties to Muladhara's history and spiritual significance. If this is your first introduction, what a lovely location to start learning about the chakras of the human spirit.

The Sacral Chakra — Svadhishthana

Moving up the spine to our second major chakra, Svadhisthana, we come upon the sacral chakra. The words translate as follows in Sanskrit: Swa means self, and adhishthana means established. This chakra is sometimes referred to as the pelvic chakra. The chakra seems to be a white lotus with six petals, each bearing a Sanskrit syllable—bam, bam, mam, yam, ram, and lam. Varuna, the ocean deity, sits in the center of the lotus, with a crescent moon shown underneath her. The sacral chakra is related to the water element, therefore this correspondence to the ocean deity makes sense. The lotus petals signify six different aspects of consciousness: attachment, pitilessness, all-destructiveness, delusion, scorn, and distrust. The second chakra is only two finger lengths away from the root chakra and can be discovered right beneath the belly button as a reference point on the body.

The sacral chakra is linked to the sense of taste and reproduction, and so to the tongue and genitals. This is your spiritual energy's emotional center, and it governs passion, pleasure, the senses, creativity, connection, and intimacy. This is where the fun is! If the root chakra is a significant and crucial chakra to humans physically, then the sacral chakra is the most serious in terms of the human condition's emotional well-being. It is a sensory information center, making it one of the most significant chakras for emotional happiness and contentment. To put it another way, if the root chakra takes care of your most basic wants such as food, shelter, and safety, the sacral chakra will ask, "How can I be happy now that my most basic needs have been met?"

This website is showing signs of excessive activity. If you intentionally engage in an unhealthy or malnourished habit, your second chakra may be out of balance. Another indicator that the sacral chakra is out of balance is emotional instability. Unhealthy relationships and codependency can develop in this setting. Anger, despair, anxiety, and overreactions are examples of other emotional disorders. Addiction is also a sign of an imbalanced second chakra. One technique to maintain this chakra balance is to ask oneself before taking any action, "Is what I'm about to do healthy for the mind or the body?" What advantages will I or others gain from the action I am about to take? "Is this healthy for me?" When the sacral chakra is blocked or congested, you may experience sadness, decreased sex drive, a loss of passion for the things that used to stimulate you, and a lack of creativity—especially if you were previously creative. One of the most common ways this chakra becomes blocked is through fear, which is strongly related to root chakra balance. These anxieties can encompass everything, but the most typical manifestations are fear of rejection or dread of death. People who are stuck in this region may spend all of their time focusing on the practical while failing to enjoy the results of their labor. Physically, blocked second chakras can cause lower back or flank pain, urinary tract or reproductive difficulties, and a lack of confidence, particularly when it comes to speaking up. Have fun while balancing an out-of-tune sacral chakra! Take some time for yourself with the express goal of enjoying it. Take a journey to somewhere you've wanted to visit for a long time. Take a bike trip around town. Make new friends by going to the neighborhood social areas. If you're more of an introvert, make some art or cook a meal you've always wanted to try. Life is designed to be enjoyed, and the sacral chakra is in charge of that enjoyment. When life's most pleasurable experiences are balanced, they are cherished without being overindulged.

Dietary support for your sacral chakra consists of eating all orange foods. When it comes to color, oranges, mangoes, peaches, carrots, apricots, and sweet potatoes all vibrate at the same frequency as the sacral chakra. Coconut water, and hydration in general, contribute to a healthy sacral chakra—after all, it is the water element chakra! Foods high in fatty omega-3 fatty acids, such as salmon, flax seed, almonds, walnuts, and sesame seed, can also aid to build the sacral chakra. These are beneficial to your cardiovascular health and inflammation.

Based on our understanding of the Kundalini, if the root chakra is where our spiritual energy is coiled and dormant, the sacral chakra Svadhishthana is where this energy manifests. Rising the Kundalini above this chakra is extremely rare because the sexual temptations that develop from this point are difficult for most yogis to overcome. Tantric saints are thought to be those who can raise their Kundalini beyond Svadhisthana.

MANIPURA IS THE SOLAR PLEXUS CHAKRA

It comes back to eating the color when it comes to fortifying Manipura through nutrition. Our color in this example is yellow. If you're searching for something savory, try bananas, maize, lemon, pineapple, and yellow curry. Complex carbs, whole grains, and legumes are also beneficial to the power chakra. Oats, rice, beans, sprouted grains, and ancient grains like faro and quinoa are high in nutrients.

ANAHATA IS THE HEART CHAKRA

You already know the drill when it comes to diet: eat your colors! In this scenario, we hear a phrase that most of us have heard before: eat your greens! Organic leafy greens are high in B vitamins, and prebiotics (the food that bacteria consume to stay healthy while inside your stomach), and can help reduce stress and enhance energy. Broccoli, kale, spinach, cucumber, peas, kiwi, lime, mint, parsley, avocado, rosemary spirulina, zucchini, chard, green apple, and green tea are among the examples. This one is quite simple to attain because so many foods contain green herbs and so many healthy foods are green. You can choose from a wide range of fruits, legumes, herbs, vegetables, leafy greens, and even tea.

VISHUDDHA (THROAT CHAKRA)

Eating blue foods helps to invigorate the throat chakra. Blueberries and even blackberries are great for balancing Vishuddha and getting your daily fiber. As an added advantage, they are high in antioxidants. Soothing foods can also help with the throat chakra. What would you eat if you woke up with a sore throat the next day? Herbal teas, raw honey, and lemon are all beneficial to the throat and its chakra. Finally, tree fruits such as apples and pears are an excellent choice.

AJNA, THE THIRD EYE CHAKRA

As we progress to the last two chakras, the color model for diet becomes hazier. We'll talk about what meals are good for the crown chakra in the next chapter, but purple foods are ideal for the third eye chakra. Grapes, purple cabbage, eggplant, and heirloom purple carrots or purple finger potatoes are excellent choices for Ajna's diet. Cocao is another excellent option; it is high in flavonoids and is a natural approach to increasing serotonin levels. Anything classified as "brain food" is beneficial to the third eye chakra. Acai is a purple food that is also considered to be one of the best superfoods on the globe. Acai tastes like a cross between blueberry and tea, maybe due to the antioxidant content of this Amazonian berry.

SAHASRARA IS THE CROWN CHAKRA

When we talk about the crown chakra and diet, we tend to focus on the detoxifying and fasting processes rather than food intake. Meditation herbs are a wonderful addition to help establish a serene mental environment conducive to profound meditation. Detoxing can help to remove toxins from the body while also increasing energy and immune system responsiveness. Crown chakra healing is primarily reliant on meditation and yoga.

THE IMPORTANCE OF CHAKRA BALANCING

Now that we know what chakras are, where these energy centers are located, and what they govern, we can move on to the most essential underlying theme: repairing them. Some of this has already been covered, such as earthing for the root chakra.

HEALING THE CHAKRA SYSTEM

So far, we've talked a lot about each of the seven fundamental chakras, including various strategies for healing and balancing these chakras along the way. We'll delve deeper into the healing process and some of the tools that can help. These gadgets can help you emit frequencies in your home, create a serene mental environment for more fruitful meditation activities, and even interact with the vibrations of specific chakras. This chapter will concentrate on crystals, essential oils, and plants that can help you become more in tune and balanced.

Essential oils can be applied in a variety of ways. They vibrate and emit a frequency in the same way that your chakras do. A diffuser, which simply adds water to the essential oils that are dispersed into the air of the space it resides in, is a common way of using essential oils. A simple technique for awakening or cleaning the energy associated with various chakras. Let's look at some of the most popular essential oils and their applications.

Lemongrass: This essential oil aids with the balance of numerous chakras, with a focus on the solar plexus chakra. Physically, this oil can help with circulation, muscle spasms or cramps, back pain, and skin toning. Emotionally, it can aid in the reduction of worry, the alleviation of past regrets or resentments, and the encouragement of optimism, positivity, and confidence. It will spiritually urge you to speak your truth and express yourself. Lemongrass is also a natural insect repellent and antibacterial.

Lavender: Promotes equilibrium in the chakras of the third, fourth, fifth, sixth, and seventh. That's nearly all of them! This makes it one of the most potent and versatile essential oils available anywhere. It will assist you in fully and efficiently expressing yourself and sharing your truth with those around you. With a stronger intuition, you may find confidence where you previously felt withdrawn or scared.

Patchouli: The root and sacral chakras are stimulated by patchouli. This essential oil enables one to appreciate their own company, to be alone with oneself, and to do so in a comfortable condition. It might help you overcome lethargy by providing you with the motivation you need to achieve your goals. It provides clarity in your desires and contentment in your existing situation. Patchouli has been shown to provide a sense of stability, prosperity, and grounding.

Frankincense: This oil stimulates the fifth chakra and teaches the user how to read energy levels in various surroundings. While working on your spiritual path in a familiar environment, it is easy to become comfortable with identifying energy. It is also crucial to apply those talents outside of the home so that you can be in tune with the energy around you no matter where you wind yourself.

Cardamom: This essential oil stimulates the second and third chakras. It is a motivational oil that boosts creativity and provides a fresh viewpoint. Working on art creation and experiencing a creative block? Use this painting to reflect on your original artistic concept, where you envisioned it heading, and possible other directions it could take if your original vision no longer works. This will also encourage working with others in a way that allows for coherence.

Spearmint: Spearmint is beneficial to the third chakra. It can boost your confidence and make you feel more strongly as you go about your day. Both spearmint and peppermint have a stress-relieving effect, and they are frequently mixed with eucalyptus oils to create a potent mixture.

Peppermint: Like its spearmint cousin, peppermint interacts with the throat chakra and is a confidence booster. The crisp, fresh aroma promotes alertness and confidence, providing you with the energy you need to complete your tasks throughout the day.

Eucalyptus: Beneficial to the fourth and fifth chakras. Eucalyptus relieves tension and anxiety by clearing the mind and allowing for clear communication and guidance.

Chamomile: Supports the second and fifth chakras. This oil aids in the comprehension of great information that spans numerous epochs. It encourages good communication and the realization of one's higher self.

Jasmine essential oils are beneficial to all chakras! The second and sixth chakras are highlighted here. It aids in the development of psychic abilities while conditioning the mind and soul to the frequency of repeated mantras. We will go through mantras in detail in the following chapter, but repetition is a vital notion to understand while discussing mantras, so train your mind to be sensitive to these repeats.

Neroli: Energetically stimulates the second and fourth chakras. This oil promotes pure love and personal light radiation. Fear fades, and hope and passion take their place. When self-love enters the picture, sorrows are swept away in its bliss. Stability and tranquillity in the user lay the groundwork for this love to flow freely.

Rosewood: Acceptance, compassion, and peace are combined with a free flow of emotion. Rosewood opens the fourth chakra. Rosewood oil plays an essential part in the health of the heart, lungs, and skin. It can aid in the releasing of repressed emotions as well as the treatment of melancholy or depression.

Sandalwood: It helps to balance your third eye chakra. This oil is ideal for meditating. It enhances self-authenticity and dispels delusions that may arise from an excessive ego. This will assist you in connecting with higher consciousness and revealing obstacles on your journey to spiritual development.

We've covered a variety of essential oils to get you started, but there are so many more available that you could write many books on the subject. To go beyond the common ones, let's look at each chakra and the essential oils that encourage a balanced vitality inside it.

Muladhara: Patchouli, Vetiver, White Lotus, Galangal, Clove, Rosemary, Cypress, Ginger, Sandalwood, Nutmeg

Svadhishthana: Orange, Myrrh, Sandalwood, Rosewood, Patchouli, Clary Sage, Bergamot, Cardamom

Manipura: Lavender, Lemon, Fennel, Juniper, Lemongrass, Black Pepper, Cinnamon, Clove, Coriander, Geranium, Ginger, Grapefruit, Cypress

Anahata: Rose, Jasmine, Ylang Ylang, Bergamot, Cypress, Geranium, Lavender, Sandalwood

Vishuddha: Peppermint, Spearmint, Eucalyptus, Camphor, Tea Tree, Bergamot, Chamomile, Basil

Ajna: Lemongrass, Lavender, Cedarwood, Patchouli, Helichrysum, Marjoram, Rosemary, Elemi

Sahasrara: Rosewood, Myrrh, Frankincense, Lavender, Helichrysum, Neroli

Finally, and maybe most significantly, research these oils and the right manner to use them before using them. Some are not designed to be applied to the skin, while others are not meant to be inhaled or consumed. This is not a how-to manual; rather, it is an introduction to the concept of employing them as a healing tool. When you locate an oil you enjoy, take precautions to ensure that you are properly utilizing its potency. There is a lot of misinformation out there, and you should exercise caution while using anything on your body.

TRANSCENDENTAL MEDITATION

Transcendental Meditation is primarily accomplished through yogic practices, meditation, and mantra repetition. In the 1950s, the Indian guru known as Maharishi Mahesh Yogi introduced this meditation technique. It became popular in the 1960s when it traveled to America, notably California. Maharishi Mahesh Yogi was particularly well-known for his association with the Beatles in India during their pursuit of spiritual growth and practices.

It has proven to be useful in reducing anxiety and assisting people in managing stress over time. Some have reported health benefits such as decreased blood pressure and a lower risk of heart problems. Unlike mindfulness-based meditations, which focus on clearing your mind of thoughts and returning your attention to the present moment when it wanders (which it will), Transcendental Meditation is centered on paying attention to a single mantra. During meditation, a mantra is a word or phrase that is silently repeated several times. Mantras are the subject of much debate, yet everyone believes that they may be tailored to each individual.

Every person's motto will be different. Those who complete training programs are frequently assigned mantras based on their personality. The mantras must be a suitable fit for the individual; otherwise, some practitioners claim that having the wrong mantras might have "dangerous" consequences.

The transcendental Meditation technique is a very gentle and natural approach to allowing your mind to achieve great peace and a state of intellectual relaxation.

During meditation, make sure your phone is turned off and that you are in a quiet place for ten to fifteen minutes. You'll need some kind of timer or a watch nearby.

Take a comfortable place and slowly close your eyes. You are free to place your hands on your lap. Just make sure you're at ease.

Choose a mantra word to employ. It is not required to make sense. It could be an insignificant word or sound. Usually two syllables. If you have a tutor, he or she can assist you in creating one. We'll use "Shiring" here, which is more of a sound than a word. It is pronounced as "Shi" and "Ring" in two syllables. While in this state, repeat this word or sound in your thoughts until it gradually sinks in. Allow it to circle your mind at whichever frequency it desires. Do not strain or force yourself.

When your mind wanders, softly bring your attention back to repeating the mantra. Allow any challenging thoughts to pass through your mind without force or judgment. Bring your attention back to the chant in your thoughts.

Continue in this manner for ten minutes. If you have a timer, wait until it goes off. After ten minutes, stop repeating the mantra in your head, sit quietly for two minutes without repeating the chant, then open your eyes and return to reality.

Transcendental meditation improves brain functioning, causing it to become more organized. This is evidenced by the physiological development of creativity and intelligence. Consistent practice of this sort of meditation improves basic memory as well. For example, schoolchildren who have been exposed to Transcendental Meditation and have done psychometric exams and choice reaction time tests typically demonstrate gains in intelligence quotient and reaction time to specific triggers. Transcendental meditation techniques also assisted them in greatly improving their basic reading, maths, study, and linguistic skills. Students in high schools, colleges, and working people have all reported an improvement in IQ.

Transcendental Meditation practice also vastly improves comprehension and the ability to focus on things, allowing one to remain awake in stressful situations. It is an excellent tool for dealing with anxiety, despair, and rage since it decreases societal pressure to engage in harmful activities.

Creativity has increased in tests of verbal and illustrative fluency, flexibility, and innovation. One becomes less influenced by assumptions and misconceptions and opens one's mind to new perspectives. After graduating, ten-year longitudinal research tracked college students who practiced meditation. The study discovered a significant rise in self-development in holistic measurements. They compared this data to graduation data sets from three control universities that were gender and age-matched. The meditators demonstrated superior moral thinking and intelligence. The meditators were also self-sufficient and well-integrated into society. This had never happened in any other group.

The Transcendental Meditation technique is unparalleled in its capacity to fully develop a person's inherent potential. This strategy helps a person become more self-reliant, more competent in dealing with obstacles, more productive, and capable of having stronger interpersonal interactions.

4 GUIDED TIBETAN MEDITATION

Tibetan Buddhism, like any other style of Buddhism, places a strong value on meditation. Because it originated in Tibet, it is known as Tibetan Meditation. It began centuries ago and was taught by Dalai Lama, a spiritual teacher who was a teacher of the Gelugpa School of Tibetan meditation in 800 B.C. The Tibetan word for meditation is 'Gom' or 'ghom,' which means "to be acquainted with one's mind." It is called this because being acquainted with the mind is the fundamental essence of meditation as a whole. According to the Dalai Lama, "The very purpose of meditation is to discipline the mind and reduce afflictive emotions."

The goal and intricacy of Tibetan meditation practices vary. The exercises, like Tibetan Buddhism itself, are impacted by borrowed characteristics of traditions from neighboring countries. Tantra, Shaivism (worship of Shiva, a supreme entity), Zen, and Indian Buddhism are among these aspects. Tibetan practices are divided into two categories: Chogom (meditation to clear the mind and produce peace) and Chaygom (meditation to explore and examine Buddhist concepts). Some of these doctrines include the Four Noble Truths, impermanence, and selflessness.

The emphasis in all Tibetan Buddhist practices is on bodhicitta, which is a state of mind inspired by a selfless yearning for all beings. Bodhicitta is thought to aid in the attainment of enlightenment. Tibetan meditation holds this in high regard and benefits much from it. The Dalai Lama, the most famous Tibetan Buddhist, described the Bodhicitta method as "wise selfishness."

Various things are utilized in Tibetan meditation to aid in full meditation. These things include mudras, which are sacred hand gestures, and mantras, which are sacred sung syllables. These, like the practices, are distinct from orthodox Buddhism. Silence and self-examination are highly valued and seen as a means of self-illumination.

There are various Tibetan meditation practices, each aiming to achieve a distinct goal in our minds.

Among these techniques are:

MAHAMUDRA MEDITATION

Mahamudra provides numerous advantages for an individual. It clears the mind. This is performed by cleansing our minds of all distracting thoughts. Mahamudra causes us to empty our minds of the past and present difficulties that are bothering us as we meditate. This, in turn, has a knock-on effect on our health since it keeps us from developing stress-related issues like high blood pressure.

. . .

It aids in the development of our best qualities. It certainly does. When we let go of negative thoughts and emotions, we become more positive and open to whatever comes our way. Our good personalities emerge from within when we have a positive mindset, and they reflect on everything we do in our work and personal lives.

Mahamudra teaches us to love and care for others. This meditation's primary goals include love and kindness. There is a lessening in animosity and filthy feelings toward others with consistent meditation. Our attitude toward living beings shifts, and we become more compassionate and loving toward them. We also cease being self-centered and start thinking about other people's needs. This moves us one step closer to enlightenment.

TUMMO MEDITATION

Tummo means 'inner fire' in the literal sense. Tibetan Buddhist monks use this traditional meditation technique. It started thousands of years ago in the Himalayas and is tantric in nature. Tummo technique combines breathing and imagery as ways for entering a profound state of meditation and boosting one's "inner heat." This inner heat aids in the regulation of body temperature. For example, keeping the body warm in chilly weather. This meditation is meant to burn away all sinful thoughts and inspire good behavior. It corrects your thoughts and stimulates positive thinking.

Tummo is one of the most widely practiced types of Buddhist practices. It is thought to be beneficial to the inner heart. Tummo meditation is popular among Buddhist adherents because it is an effective approach to developing self-control. If you ever go to a

Buddhist monastery, you will undoubtedly learn a lot about Tummo Meditation.

Wim Hof is a well-known example of someone who has reaped the benefits of Tummo meditation. He is known as the 'Iceman' because he is fearless and unyielding. This was due to his amazing ability to withstand cold. He was the first person to run barefoot through the Arctic and is currently aiming for Antarctica! What could be crazier than that? He once spent seventy-three minutes immersed in an ice bath. He enjoys pushing his body to its limits, especially in frigid conditions. He also attempted to conquer Mount Everest while wearing only shorts. Isn't that crazy? However, he holds more than 15 world records due to his incredible ability to withstand the ice.

To begin Tummo meditation, sit on a mat. Cross your legs by crossing one leg over the other. Place your hands on your knees and close your eyes.

Concentrate on yourself and eliminate all bad thoughts from your mind. Avoid forming ideas that bombard you from all sides and damage your thinking. You should not entertain any nasty or wicked thoughts.

There are noticeable motions in the bowel when you breathe. It gradually rises and falls. As you inhale and exhale, keep your attention on the bowel movement.

Bring your gaze upwards, concentrating on the nose. Take note of your breathing as you inhale and exhale.

When you reach that level of concentration without being distracted by thoughts, see your body as hollow in your mind.

With consistent practice, you will be able to rekindle that inner fire.

This meditation is a good method for opening up the chakras. The practice's primary purpose is to clear the chakras to achieve enlightenment. It makes it easier to enter the dominant channel, resulting in exceptional happiness and clarity of being. This state, also known as enlightenment, is easily recognized as our actual essence. Beginners achieve excellent results in this as well.

Tummo meditation promotes inner contentment. It aids in the development of a pleasant and blissful personality. This inner happiness might also aid in the recovery from addiction. If the addiction is motivated by a need for pleasure, the euphoria of inner fire dwarfs all other forms of pleasure. This inner happiness is the cultivation of the enigmatic inner delight experienced in Kundalini energy that differs from exterior pleasures like sex or eating your favorite dish. This energy can be developed anywhere, at any moment, such as while driving. It is also useful when you are feeling cold or frightened. This inner happiness produces a palpable heat from within.

The Tummo method reduces impediments as well. It ignites a great inner energy that triumphs over the ego and takes control. Regular practice of this meditation is thought to quickly erase impediments to spiritual and worldly enlightenment. Tummo meditation is taught at Buddhist schools at the end of the Vajrayana path, which is a fast track to enlightenment. It has historically been kept secret and only handed to the highest advanced students throughout time. However, many reputable teachers advise that powerful techniques like these should be made available to the general people to counteract bad influences in these turbulent times.

Tummo is an excellent instrument for developing confidence and power. In yoga, it opens the second chakra, which is related to physical power, creativity, and sexuality. It assists the meditator in constructively focusing and using nervous energy to clear confusion and increase confidence. This method is used in martial arts to help martial artists pull strength for incredible feats of balance and strength. It aids them in breaking through cement blocks with their attacks. The entire focus of Tai Chi is on developing beautiful and flawless balance movements. Connecting to this inner power allows you to harness the power to fulfill all of your objectives and dreams, as well as attain your full potential.

MEDITATION WITH TONGLEN

Tong means "letting go" and len means "accepting." Tonglen practice is thus a way of engaging with our own and others' pain. Everyone has an inbuilt fear of adversity and suffering. Tonglen practice assists in conquering fear and releasing tension in our souls. It awakens the compassion that exists in all of us, no matter how callous or frigid we appear to be.

For example, you could be having a tense dispute with your supervisor or your spouse at work. They're yelling at you, and you're at a loss for words. You might start by breathing in pain and exhaling a sense of calm and freshness. This relaxing breath is for you, the person yelling at you, and everyone else dealing with a stressful circumstance. Of course, you must respond to the person's ranting, but adding some distance and love into the situation will help you handle it more skillfully.

Tonglen is a four-stage formal meditation practice:

Begin by shining on absolute bodhichitta. This is accomplished by briefly resting your thoughts in a condition of quiet for a second or two. This stage allows us to experience basic freshness and clarity.

Second, experiment with texture. Breathe in a heated and heavy sense of claustrophobia, and breathe out a cold and light sense of refreshment. Breathe in and out until everything feels in sync.

Third, deal with a personally difficult problem that you are familiar with. People usually start by doing tonglen for someone they care about and want to aid. However, if you are focused on your particular anguish, you can conduct the exercise for the agony you are experiencing as well as for all people experiencing similar suffering. For example, if you're feeling inadequate, breathe it in for yourself and everyone else who feels the same way. Send out confidence, relief, and adequacy in whichever way you want.

Finally, broaden the scope of the process. For example, if you are practicing Tonglen for someone you care about, extend it to others who are in the same situation as your friend. If you're performing Tonglen for a distant acquaintance, do the same for others in a similar situation. Make it bigger than just you and someone else. Tonglen is large enough if you do it for everyone who has comparable emotions to you, such as rage or fear. However, in all of these circumstances, you could always go further. Tonglen could be done for persons who have wounded you or others--those you regard to be your foes. Consider them to be folks in the same perplexed and trapped predicament as you or your acquaintance. Take in their anguish and send them relief.

Tonglen, like all meditation techniques, provides benefits. It keeps us continually appreciative of what we have. It aids in eliminating the world of misery and cultivating compassion in ourselves. As you practice this meditation, pay attention to the distress of people you know or even those you don't know, such as people who are internally displaced in their nations due to war. In any case, it serves as a nice reminder of how fortunate we are and of the things we should cherish in this life.

Tonglen also reminds us of the tremendous power of Karma. Indeed, we have all had firsthand experience with events that demonstrate how doing good in the world benefits us. Taking in the misery of others and bringing happiness into their lives is a continuous practice of a type of Karma that brings more positivity into the world.

This meditation practice can assist you in dealing with difficult individuals and situations. Tonglen meditation can be your key to finding calm when dealing with challenging people that create stressful situations in your life. You can practice taking in and exhaling your stress, as well as taking in the negativity of those tough individuals around you. This helps everyone find the peace they seek.

It has the potential to alter your connection. Yes, it is possible! Tonglen can significantly alter your interactions with others and transform your connections with them. Even if you are unaware of it. It can make you more understanding and caring. It may also cause you to recall them more frequently.

Tonglen also aids in the healing of pain. Tonglen meditation's primary purpose is to achieve this. It alleviates both your own and others' pain. It is effective at this. You can make a significant difference in the world by absorbing negative energy and replacing it with positive energy.

Tonglen practice can help you improve spiritually. This is the most significant advantage of Tonglen meditation. If you use this approach regularly, you will experience spiritual growth in ways you never imagined possible.

MEDITATION USING MANDALAS

Mandala is a Sanskrit term that means "sacred circle." Mandalas are circular motifs that represent the never-ending nature of life. Many mandalas contain a spiritual component. In many spiritual traditions, the mandala is a symbol of completeness in life and is utilized as a focal point for meditation and contemplation. The Hindus were the first to fully use the mandala as a technique for meditation. However, Buddhists popularized the ritual and extended it throughout the world. The mandala allows the meditator to feel aligned and linked to the universe. Creating a mandala in the sacred circle is a deeper process that can awaken you to the energy core of your true self and open you up to great healing.

Mandalas can be found throughout nature, including the Earth, moon, and sun. Individuals, on the other hand, might construct them to assist symbolize life's remarkable and lovely path. Mandalas can also reveal the story of a person's former life.

Various sorts of mandalas express various messages. They can be Flower Mandalas, which often include a flower in bloom. This is demonstrated by the circles being filled with repeating petals and complicated shapes. Butterfly, bee, ladybug, and dragonfly patterns are possible. They typically represent femininity, fertility, harmony, and eternity.

Geometric Mandalas are lovely mandalas made of intertwined geometric motifs that appear in recurring patterns. Ovals and circles, as well as triangular and rectangular shapes, are examples of shapes. Geometric mandalas allow for a lot of color experimentation.

Celestial Mandalas incorporate heavenly bodies like the moon, sun, and stars. They are visually appealing and eye-catching. They can signify several characteristics such as knowledge, spiritual enlightenment, or eternity. They are frequently adopted by different tribes and take on tribal cultural emblems.

Religious Mandalas are mandalas that are made to look like traditional Buddhist mandalas. They may occasionally include religious or sectarian symbols. In Christianity, the emblems may include a cross, a dove, or any other Christian symbol. The background could be a dawn or a heavenly scene. These mandalas may appeal to religious people.

Nature mandalas, on the other hand, frequently incorporate a plethora of pictures portraying nature. These photographs show coastlines, hills, and wildflower fields. These mandalas may assist you in connecting with the natural world around you.

Mandalas come in a variety of colors and shapes. Red mandalas, for example, represent strength, great energy, and passion. Orange mandalas are associated with creativity, self-awareness, and intuition. Green mandalas represent physical healing, nature love, cognitive ability, and care, whereas blue mandalas represent emotional healing, meditation, and inner harmony.

When meditating with the mandala, place the chosen mandala at arm's length in front of you on a table or the floor.

Mandalas have been shown to boost concentration. When you concentrate on the act of coloring mandalas, your brain can turn off from the constant flow of thoughts in your head. When a mandala represents something personal to you, it might help you focus on and improve those ideas in your life.

They also foster creative expression. Coloring-prepared mandalas allow for freedom of expression within a safe framework. This could be useful for folks who enjoy creating art but lack the ability or confidence to create creative works of art.

Mandalas provides tranquillity and peace. Everyone is juggling numerous duties. Nonetheless, mental health should not be overlooked in any of these activities. Mandala coloring can provide you with a sense of relief after a long day. They can also aid with concentration because coloring the patterns requires attention and serenity. This deep involvement in coloring relieves tension and reduces anxiety.

They also strengthen the immune system. This benefit is incredible. Mandalas, according to modern medicine, create serenity and have become a healing aid. Mandalas improve concentration, promote sound sleep, and alleviate discomfort, thereby improving the immune system.

Mandalas bring out our inner child. Coloring mandala pages for inner child healing treatment helps you break all forms of negative thinking patterns by reconnecting you with your inner child. This encourages grownups to appreciate themselves more and become better people. It also increases self-esteem and helps one handle the hardships of life.

MEDITATION ON SHAMATHA

Shamatha is another name for calm-abiding meditation. The Tibetan meditation technique, also known as calm-abiding meditation, has been achieving mental one-pointedness since ancient times. This is extraordinary and necessitates a trip to achieve perfect clarity, simplicity, and pure force. This is attained by consistent and devout practice, as well as the development of Shamatha meditation.

Tibetan Buddhist tradition sees the process of quiet abiding as 'the way', dating back to Buddha's ancient teachings. This practice of peaceful abiding meditation is ideal for beginners and aids in the development of a strong, solid, and healthy connection.

This meditation is unique and special in that it also gives a very stimulating and motivating manner for gradual evolution, making it particularly desirable to advanced meditators.

The goal of peaceful abiding meditation is to constantly return your attention to the target of meditation. Breath is always a good focal point, but any comfortable object can be used. Calm-abiding allows you to acquire the capacity of your mind and get more control over the energy of your ideas and emotions. Calm-abiding eventually opens up a much more evenly centered mind.

Calm abiding combines mind balancing and transcendence of dual thought. There is a sequence of distracting thoughts while meditating, as when we are trying to settle into a session, there is a wave of thoughts that takes time to settle.

The route of quiet abiding is a long and progressive journey that must be appreciated. The first step of calm-abiding begins as one prepares to begin calm abiding while settling into an object of focus.

Calm-abiding is accomplished in phases, the first of which is Placing the Mind. The meditator's goal during this entering phase is to find an object. As previously said, the breath is an excellent focal point because it is based on the present moment. Once the object is located and the meditation session begins, the mind travels all over the place, making it difficult to locate the object among the swirling thoughts in your mind. To find the thing, one must concentrate completely. However, the mind will go in and out of focus for the majority of the session.

Continuity Stage of placement. When we are eventually able to focus our minds on an object and hold them there for a short period, there is continuity where there was none previously.

Stage of patch-like placement. This is a stage in which one may maintain attention on an object for an extended period. Though the focus is lost from time to time, the meditator can refocus his or her attention on the item for a longer period.

Stage of close placement. From the start until the finish of the session, the item is never lost at this stage. Though distraction and boredom persist, one component of the mind can maintain a continuous flow of persistent attention.

Controlling Stage of placement. When one becomes acquainted with stage 4 and achieves that steadiness, there is a tremendous sense of inner calm. This is a sense I've never felt before. The mind has been like a kettle of boiling water up to this point, and when it finally settles down, the deeper mind achieves serenity. This produces a strong sense of pleasure.

Stage of calm. This level is harder to perceive when deep in meditation, but it is quite present at the moment. This is the power of clinging to an object. There are, nevertheless, minor variances in excitement and dullness.

Completely calming stage. This entire session lacks excitement, expectation, and distraction. Even if they do arise, the meditator has perfect control and can make even the smallest disruption vanish instantaneously. This is the point at which the 'ordinary mind' gives way to the 'calm abiding' mind. The mind is alive, energetic, and focused here.

Stage with a single point. With everyday practice, the meditator will be able to enter a fixed meditation much more easily than before.

Stage of Fixed Absorption or Meditative Equipoise. This is the point at which the ego and any sense of need are transcended. The 'quiet abiding' mind is polished and sustained over time by extensive and repetitive practice. When the mind and body are fully grown and connected, there is a profound revolution and freedom. This is the experience of ecstasy and joy, which is accompanied by mental sharpness and physical lightness.

We don't know how dispersed, depressing, uninteresting, and preoccupied our brains are until we achieve Shamatha. Then we discover how potent the focused mind is. The mind is like a muscle, and Shamatha is like a muscle-building workout. If you practice Shamatha as an athlete, you will improve and become a better athlete; if you practice Shamatha as a musician, you will become a better musician. If you are a spiritual, mystical person who practices Shamatha, you will move quickly down the path.

MEDITATION THROUGH VISUALIZATION

Visualization is also known as mental imagery or mental rehearsal. It is a strategy that helps you to feel the emotions associated with reaching a future objective. Because its roots are in visual pictures and other sense practices, it is a technique akin to guided visualization.

A traditional Tibetan Buddhist practice involves imagining a core figure, generally a deity, from which numerous additional figures emerge. When all of these people come, they are absorbed back into the primary figure, who is then absorbed back into the meditator.

It can take the form of a film or kinesthetic perspective. You may vividly recall sensations in your body, as well as the action and its effects. You can see a scene, another person, or a sequence of events when doing a simple visualization. Something other than yourself. You can imagine yourself in a situation and feel the effects on your body and mind.

The ultimate purpose of this technique is to realize that all things are illusions created by our imagination. Before they are reabsorbed, the central and accompanying figures must be awakened to their emptiness.

The answer to living in a condition of dream illusion, according to Tibetan practice, is to reabsorb the inner personalities back into the mind. Indeed, it is similar to modern therapeutic psychology in that it encourages us to make unconscious content conscious. The fundamental lesson of Tibetan practice is that it is only when our ideas are recognized as self or not the self that they become independent figures. To absorb them, we must first start the process by acknowledging that the inner faces in our thoughts are not real persons, but rather our imagination. This permits us to accept and absorb thoughts that we previously rejected or sent out into the world.

It is usually tough to maintain focus the first time this strategy is utilized. People are easily sidetracked by random or negative thoughts or their environment. Persistence, as usual, pays off, and someone gradually acquires a stronger ability to benefit from meditation.

The following procedures will assist you in visualizing during meditation:

Concentrate on mental exercise. Use any of the numerous concentration exercises to begin the meditation. Taking deep, regulated breaths helps you stay calm and focused on something other than your troubles. Another approach is to direct your gaze and focus on an object. Whatever emphasis you choose will guide you through the rest of the visualizing process.

Concentrate on one aspect of your life. You may dislike certain aspects of your life. Do not attempt to repair them all at once. Instead, concentrate on a single part of your life, such as your work, relationships, financial condition, or a life function such as being a spouse.

Consider the best-case scenario. Now, consider the best-case scenario. Not just that, but picture it clearly and in great detail.

Negative thoughts should be allowed to pass. Allow your anxieties, fears, and disputes to pass without focusing on them. You can't stop your mind from thinking. You may, however, deny them the ability to remain in your head.

Consider a Mid-Range Goal. Consider a period in the not-too-distant future when you will have made progress toward your objective. Consider your mid-term target. Consider the steps you are taking or will take to move toward your anticipated future.

Consider your life after achieving that aim. Next, visualize what your life will be like once you've completed that SMART objective. Consider it carefully. Consider how you'll feel emotionally.

Take a step back and take in the scenery. Now, take a step back and observe yourself, as if you were watching television, experiencing that fantastic feeling and thrilling sensations associated with reaching your goal. Delight in the fact that you have already made a vital step toward making your dream a reality.

Return to the center to select quick steps toward your objective. Finally, return your attention to the actions you will take in the coming day, week, or month as propulsion toward achieving your goal. Take note of these short-term SMART goals and consider their ability to guide you to success. Close your visualization meditation by relaxing into your physical self and feeling the sensations in your current environment.

You may be imagining what this incredible approach could achieve for your life. Perhaps you've seen a few advantages.

Visualization, on the other hand, aids in stress reduction. Are you feeling off-kilter? Visualization is one of the most effective strategies to refocus your attention. Visualizing your day aids in the organization of your ideas, mental preparation, and stress reduction. Listening to calm music enhances the experience.

Boost motivation. Motivational visualization entails imagining moments of accomplishment and the feelings that come with them. Kindle all of your senses and immerse yourself in mental images until it appears real to you. Familiarizing yourself with sensations of accomplishment increases your motivation to achieve your ultimate goal as well as your notion that success is more conceivable and realistic.

5 GUIDED ZEN MEDITATIONS

Zen meditations, often known as 'Zazen', are sitting meditation techniques. Zazen means "seated meditation" in Japanese. It is a frequent practice profoundly entrenched in Buddhist consciousness that both beginners and masters observe. Mudras (Hand postures), state of mind, and body position are all factors in Zazen meditation, as they are in all other meditations.

As much as Zazen is centered on sitting, not all sitting positions are the same. This meditation uses several positions to achieve various meditation goals. Half Lotus (Hankafuza), in which the meditator places the left foot on the right thigh, is one of these positions. It is difficult to adopt comfortably at first, but with consistent practice, it becomes simpler. Burmese Position: Knees flat on the floor, one ankle in front of the other; and Kneeling Position (Sezia), in which practitioners kneel and rest their hips on their ankles.

A Zafu, or meditation cushion, is also required in Zen meditation positions. This style of cushion promotes excellent posture and gives comfort. This is critical since it will be tough to focus if you do not get a decent, comfortable posture. And you won't get the full benefits of meditation if you don't focus.

If you cannot obtain a Zafu, you can use a rolled-up blanket for support. The importance of comfort cannot be overstated. There are also Zen-appropriate chairs.

Zen includes a variety of techniques. These strategies are practiced in a variety of ways and achieve a variety of aims.

MEDITATION AT HUA-T'OU

Hua-T'ou means "head of speech." The term Hua-t'ou can also be translated as a "critical phrase" in Chinese. Hua-t'ou is also known as hwadu and wato in Korean and Japanese. A hua-t'ou is a brief phrase (often part of a koan) that can be used as a meditation and introspection anchor. It helps to focus the mind in a specific way, which contributes to enlightenment.

The phrase (huatou) is generally considered as a question or an interrogative sentence in Huatou meditation. The meditators are advised to ask themselves the question (huatou) continually to produce a sense of self doubt (yiqing) or the emotion of "I don't know." A hua-t'ou is always short and stands alone.

Over time, there has been extensive evidence that focusing on this type of doubt sensation usually leads meditators through different meditation levels, increasing their Zen experience, and discovering their true, enlightened nature.

Though not often practiced in Western Zen circles, this type of meditation is widely used in Korean and Chinese Zen. Since the late-life discovery of hua-t'ou meditation by the famed Korean monk Chinul (1158-1210), it has been a popular kind of meditation practice among Korean Zen monks until this day. In China, the practice dates back to before the 11th century. Hsu-Yun (1840-1959), a notable Zen monk of the 19th and 20th centuries, routinely practiced and taught hua-t'ou meditation as his favorite kind of meditation practice.

The hua-t'ou, though popular centuries ago, is still a valuable method for people today. It is not necessary to have regular meetings with an instructor or a group of individuals. It can be done at any time during the day, not only when sitting. As a result, it gives more time for Zen practice, whether at home or the office.

There are numerous Hua-t'ou.

Some well-known examples include "Who is repeating the Buddha's name?"

This hua-t'ou is quite popular among Chinese people. Those who frequently sing Amitabha Buddha's name, in particular. Chanting this name is a Pureland practice, based on devoutness and faith in Amitabha Buddha, which leads to a restored rebirth. This hua-t'ou transforms Zen practice into a search for enlightenment in this lifetime.

"Who is it that is dragging this corpse around?" Hsu-Yun popularized this huo-t'ou in current times. According to his autobiography, it was given to him by his Tian-tai sect Master Yang-jing. He then taught it to many others as their first lesson.

"Who exactly am I?" The great 20th century Indian teacher Ramana Maharshi utilized this statement as a focal point for meditation with his followers. He, on the other hand, exploited it in a variety of ways.

This technique can be carried out in a variety of ways. Each method is determined by the teacher's background and personal experience.

When performing hua-t'ou, choose a hua-tou. Most professors will select a hua-tou for their students. It is not strictly necessary, but it is really useful. Unless your teacher knows you well, you are the best judge of your hua-t'ou. Once you've chosen your hua-tou, don't change it. Do not be concerned if you believe you made the wrong choice. Keep going with it. If you delve far enough into the hua-tou, you will discover that they are ultimately all the same.

Begin using this hua-tou during your meditation hour. Maintain a regular meditation routine. It's required for hua-t'ou meditation. Create a meditation routine, whether it's once a day or once a week. Routines are difficult to establish and need a great deal of discipline. Make no excuses for not doing them.

Throughout the day, work on your hua-tou. Include it in all of your activities. You can practice it while driving, cooking, doing laundry, or doing anything else. It's best to include it in tasks that don't require your undivided concentration.

Take note of the outcomes. Your concentration and awareness will grow stronger over time. Noticing these changes, like noticing the results of working out, helps us persist with the activity.

The hua-t'ou practice necessitates extensive knowledge of the Three Greats. These are Great Willpower, Great Faith, and Great Doubt.

Great Determination: We must be determined to awaken to our actual nature and know who we truly are. We must recognize the significance of this determination and recognize the constant pressing need to tackle the situation.

We must have great faith in the effectiveness of hua-t'ou meditation. We must think that this practice has been carried out by many people in the past and now, and that it has resulted in positive outcomes for them. Most essential, we must believe that it will work well for us.

Great Doubt: developing doubt is a major component of this approach. Ta-Hui fostered the development of strong skepticism. Because of its power to transform one into a creative thinker, he placed uncertainty at the heart of the hua-t'ou practice. Doubt is the beginning and end of hua-t'ou practice. It is entirely founded on the formation of doubt and, as a result, the acquisition of insight.

MEDITATION WITH KOANS

A koan is a conundrum or riddle used by Zen Buddhists during meditation. It enables someone to discover higher truths about the world and himself. They resemble the hua-t'ou but differ somewhat.

Koan is a Japanese word that sounds a lot like "gongan" in Chinese, which means "public case." In ancient times, "public case" meant "open case" in a legal sense. It meant being completely open for everyone to view, test, and criticize one's comprehension of Zen.

Most experiences with Koans included a dialogue meeting between the Zen master and the individual involved in the Koan discussion, who was usually a Zen student. It occasionally included an amateur. Koans can be complicated stories with wordplay, screams, or even physical beating or kicking between the teacher and the pupil. These forms of Koans are typically identified through existing Koan collections such as The Blue Cliff Record (Hekiganroku), The Gateless Gate (Mumonkan), or where Koans are presented alongside a lyrical overview and comprehensive commentary. This demonstrates the tiny difference between the Koan and the Hua T'ou, as the Koan is performed in public.

The koan's foundation is to drain the critical and egoist mind to reveal the more intuitive no-mind. Their goal does not always have to be to find a solution. They are intended to make us realize the limitations of our minds and how they can never supply us with a satisfactory solution. Some argue that Koans act against the intellect. They are, however, neither intellectual nor anti-intellectual. They only highlight the fact that reality cannot be grasped. Two of the most famous koans are basic, brief, to the point, and elegant.

"When both hands clap, a sound is produced; listen to the sound of one hand clapping." "Also, what exactly is Buddha?" "Three pounds of flax," you say.

As humans, we enjoy deciphering the meaning of every speech we hear. We will sometimes go to considerable efforts to find meaning in a collection of words. However, more often than not, we will pick the simplest path to understanding. As a rule, we prefer solutions that are less mentally challenging. This leaves a lot of possibilities for misunderstandings, but it's also how our minds are wired as humans. Taking the time to understand phrases is the business of academics and poets, not commoners. But we still want to know what message the other person is trying to express. The koan is opposed to such understanding communication.

Individual experience is required to comprehend the meaning of a koan, but it is also widely thought about and shared in a communal environment. That is the public face of the "public case." Working with koans allows us to actualize our embodiment of the collective understanding passed down to us over the millennia. The playing field of the koan is not restricted to ourselves, but when we encounter the gap left by enormous regions of thinking and experience varied sentiments in response to the moment.

What makes koans so fascinating and beautiful is that they are not intended to define or even teach us anything, but rather to inspire us to incorporate them into our lives to experience a similar state of consciousness as the characters in the particular story.

When first trying to understand a koan, don't push yourself too hard. Continue to repeat the koan's phrases to yourself, something like, "The coin that's lost in the river is found in the river." By doing so, you initiate an ongoing dialogue with the koan and build an intimate relationship with it. This is so you can sit back and relax while everything happens.

Allow the koan to enter your current existence. Consider it a game. Everyone wants to learn meditation as a skill, yet taking the time to learn a skill reduces the size of your life. It is quite personal. Something in your life will come up and meet the lost coin. It will not be a surprise, and it will not be what you expected.

Place your faith in the unknown. Allow the koan to transform you. Normally, if we want to learn more about anything, we take it to the top floor and look for a particular shelf with a label for it. When we prioritize meditation, we step outside of our own lives. Accept and integrate the koan into your entire being. Into your heart and soul.

Play around with the koan. Try out the koan, make mistakes, discover its virtues, misunderstand it, and experiment with it. A koan can never be broken. As with the coin koan, ask yourself questions such as "Is this a coin?" "Is there anything lost?"

The most important thing to remember when meditating on a koan is to refrain from passing judgment, criticism, or finding fault with whatever comes to mind. This covers how you're progressing with the koan. Don't condemn yourself if you do judge, criticize, and find fault with yourself. Accept it instead, and compassion will follow.

Meditating on a koan not only provides the advantages of meditation but also provides your mind with a vigorous mental workout. Athletes benefit from fitness. Meditating on a koan opens your eyes to yourself and the nature and fauna around you in a new way.

6 YOGA POSES

As you can see, Buddhism includes a variety of practices aiming towards enlightenment. Yoga is one of these techniques. Yoga literally means "union." It is essentially a spiritual discipline founded on an incredibly subtle science that focuses on bringing mind and body into harmony. It is both an art and a science to live a healthy life. Yoga, according to Yogic teachings, leads to the union of individual consciousness with Universal awareness. This represents the perfect coordination of the mind and body, Man and Nature.

This union can be understood on several levels: Philosophically, it is a merger of the virtual, partial self and the absolute Self. In religion, it is viewed as the union of the particular soul with the infinite spirit. Psychologically, as personality integration - a state in which a person no longer lives at odds with himself - as the calming of the waves of likes and dislikes, allowing oneself to stay complete in himself in all circumstances.

Yoga has a long history, however there are numerous incidents of anonymity and uncertainty. This is owing to the mysterious character of its teachings and the oral transmission of sacred texts. Yoga's early writings were kept on delicate palm leaves that were easily destroyed or lost. Yoga, on the other hand, can be traced back over 5,000 years, and some academics believe it may be as old as 10,000 years. According to legend, Lord Shiva was the first instructor of Yoga. Yoga is widely regarded as a 'immortal cultural outcome' of the Indus Valley civilization, which dates back to 2700 B.C. and has proven to cater to both physical and spiritual elevating of humanity. Yoga Sadhana's very identity is based on basic humanitarian values.

Over 5,000 years ago, the Indus-Sarasvati civilization in Northern India pioneered the creation of Yoga. Yoga was originally referenced in the Rig Veda, India's oldest sacred literature. The Vedas were a collection of manuscripts comprising hymns, chants, and rituals used by Vedic priests known as Brahmans. Yoga was gradually advanced by the Brahmans and Rishis (mystic seers) who documented their practices and ideas in the Upanishads, a massive work spanning over 200 scriptures. The most famous of the Yogic scriptures is the Bhagavad-Gîtâ, which was written approximately 500 B.C.E. The Upanishads embraced and adapted the Vedic concept of ceremonial sacrifice, training on ego sacrifice through self-knowledge, action, and wisdom.

A yogi (sometimes spelled Jogi) is a yoga practitioner.

There are numerous forms of yoga available, whether you prefer a more intense, demanding practice or a gentle, peaceful, and calming class. Depending on the teacher, each style differs slightly from the others. I recommend trying out a few different styles with the teachers before picking on your favorite. Even if you're a seasoned yogi with a lot of skill and flexibility, any of the following styles could improve your overall yoga experience and push you beyond of your comfort zone.

Yoga styles include the following:

YOGA HATHA

Hatha means "force" in Sanskrit. The breath, body, and mind are all involved in the practice. Its lessons typically last 45 to 90 minutes and include breathing exercises, yoga positions, and meditation. Hatha yoga breathing practices can be found in Buddhist and Hindu scriptures dating back to the first century. It took another 1,000 years, however, for yoga poses, or asanas, and breath control to be documented as a means to promote bright energy.

Classical Hatha yoga was founded in the 15th century and included instructions for the proper placement of yoga poses or asanas, pranayama or breathing exercises, mudras or hand gestures, and meditation for personal spiritual growth.

This type of yoga typically entails physical activities to settle the body, mind, and soul in preparation for greater spiritual activity. Because 'Ha' means sun and 'Tha' means moon, Hatha yoga seeks to align the solar and lunar forces within you in order to gain more mental calm. Regular hatha yoga asana practice can help practitioners develop a strong body and mind, allowing them to achieve inner bliss. Furthermore, Hatha yoga is a crucial step toward the balance of a person's masculine and feminine parts, which increases your consciousness. Aside from the regular practice of yoga postures aimed at improving your physical, mental, emotional, and spiritual well-being, the hatha yoga program includes correct diet intake.

There are various asanas in hatha Yoga.

STANDING FORWARD BEND POSE (UTTANASANA)

Stand on a yoga mat with your spine straight and your hands on your hips. Take a deep breath and raise your arms toward the ceiling. Exhale by bending at the hips and bringing your arms to the floor next to each foot. You can also place your hands on the back of your ankles. Rest your thigh on your chest, nose, and forehead. Hold this position for around 15-20 seconds. The hamstrings and calves are stretched in this hatha yoga posture. It also helps to strengthen the thighs and knees, alleviates headaches and anxiety, and is beneficial for asthma and high blood pressure.

(SETU BANDHASANA) BRIDGE POSE

Lie on your back with your legs bent and your arms on the floor. Bring your heels tight to your back and press your feet firmly into the ground. Lift your posterior and chest, then your lower back, as you exhale. Relax your neck and head on the floor after moving your shoulder blades away from your ears. Join your hands underneath your back. Maintain this position for 30-60 seconds. This pose, when practiced regularly, expands the heart, chest, and shoulders. It also massages the spine, neck, thighs, and back pleasantly.

Begin in a raised position with feet hip-distance apart in Tree Pose (Vrikshasana). Maintain a solid grip on the floor and elevate your left leg high. Place the left foot on the inner thigh of the right. Align your left and right posteriors. Maintain your posture, take a few deep breaths, and try to balance your body. Fold your palms in front of your chest in the Namaste position and quietly glance forward. Maintain this position for 30-60 seconds. The goal of Tree Pose is to extend the thighs, shoulders, and groins. It tones the abdominal muscles and has been reported to be beneficial for back ailments such as sciatica.

YOGA VINYASA

Vinyasa is also known as "flow" because of the ease with which the poses flow together. It is one of the most popular modern yoga methods. It's a broad category that includes many various forms of yoga, including Ashtanga.

Vinyasa is the polar opposite of Hatha in modern yoga terminology. Hatha sessions often concentrate on one pose at a time, with breaks in between. Vinyasa classes, on the other hand, thread numerous poses together to form a sequence. The sequence can be fixed, as in Ashtanga, where the poses are always performed in the same order. However, most of the time, Vinyasa teachers have the freedom to arrange the development of poses in their own way.

Each action in vinyasa yoga corresponds to a breath. The breath takes precedence, acting as an anchor as you transition from one pose to the next.

Vinyasa allows for a lot of variation, although it almost always includes sun salutations. Expect to move quickly from one stance to the next. The unique teacher and the particular style in which he or she is training will determine whether the class is rapid or slow, offers advanced poses, or is very alignment oriented.

Some courses begin with warm-up stretches, while others get right into standing positions. Some prominent yoga methods are also classified as vinyasa. Jivamukti, Core-power, Baptiste Power Vinyasa, and Modo are among them. If a class is just called vinyasa, it may combine elements from several distinct traditions. The fluidity between poses is the one thing you can be confident of.

CAT-COW POSE (CHAKRAVAKASANA)

This is a very important and motivating yoga stance. It entails shifting the spine from a rounded to an arched position. Each movement is performed in tandem with an inhalation or exhalation of the breath. This is a simple vinyasa position since the breath is linked to the movement. This pose can be done as part of a warm-up sequence, a recreation sequence, or as a back-pain prevention exercise.

Arching and extending the spine can aid enhance flow in your back's discs. It's a simple movement, but it can be quite effective in supporting the back, relieving discomfort, and maintaining a healthy spine.

Cat-Cow Stretch might help you improve your posture and balance if you spend a lot of time sitting. Because the movements are linked to your breathing, it is also said to be an excellent stress reliever and calming pose.

SALUTATION TO THE SUN

Sun salutations are an important component of any vinyasa flow-style yoga practice. Many professors utilize them as warm-ups at the start of class, and others even base entire classes on them. Learning this sequence can be really beneficial, particularly if you wish to practice at home. One of the most difficult aspects of practicing yoga alone is determining what to do when you first go onto your mat. Sun salutations, on the other hand, offer a clear remedy.

This series relies heavily on the breath. The transition from one pose to the next is always done in tandem with an intake or exhale of the breath. The amount of breaths in each pose can be changed to influence the tempo of the routine. Only make sure to move to the next pose on the correct breath every time.

YOGA FOR TAOISTS

Taoist Yoga is mainly based on one of the oldest Chinese spiritual systems. It is a contemporary kind of yoga that incorporates Taoist traditions and Indian cultural practices. The Tao Yin practice is based on faith in the Tao, or the Way. On the surface, this is one of life's invisible realities. It can allude to things we take for granted, such as the change of seasons, the rising tides, human breathing, and the entire cycle of life.

What exactly is this Way? The Way is separated into two halves, one of which is defined as fiery, aggressive, dominant, and potent. The other half is the polar opposite of the first - soft, nurturing, and subservient. This is the concept of Yin and Yang. The Way is made up of the confluence of these two opposing conceptions that are mutually dependant.

Tao Yoga was created by Tao Yin in order to develop and promote the Tao Way via loving, gentle motions, and exercises. Early Tao Yin scholars and followers employed these exercises to improve their health and devote their life to a deeper comprehension of the Way.

As is customary, the breath plays an important role in this phase. Moving from one pose to the next is always done in tandem with an inhale or exhale of the breath. You can change the pace of the routine by varying the amount of breaths in each pose.

Taoist yoga is related to Tai Chi. Despite certain sophisticated movements derived from the Hatha yoga and Tai Chi roots, Taoist yoga is regarded as a relatively straightforward way for thoroughly understanding the body and the self. It is claimed to have three main objectives:

First and foremost, Taoist yoga was created to help its practitioners grow a stronger and more flexible physique. It enables the acquisition of a healthy, toned body, which is necessary for improving bodily conditions. This is true not only in the physical sense, but also in the mental and spiritual.

The Taoist Yoga practice then seeks to assist the practitioner become more aware of the relationship between the mind, the body, and the way they breathe.

Finally, it seeks to expand the follower's spiritual energy, which flows within the body and nourishes both the individual and the universe's vitality.

These objectives are significant because they are said to promote self-healing in the yogi, achieve a balance between the body and the mind, and increase physical strength. All of these objectives demonstrate Taoist yoga as an ideal practice for improving well-being on all levels.

Taoist Yoga provides numerous advantages for the practitioner. Aside from giving the body strength and improving balance, one can enjoy benefits such as enhanced flexibility and stamina -

including sexual stamina, better sleep at night, an improved immune system, and a slowing of the aging process.

Taoist yoga focuses not just on fitness but also on a person's overall growth.

It is thus advised for anyone seeking a holistic balance of body, mind, and spirit.

BONUS INCLUDED: 30 MINUTES OF GUIDED MEDITATION

Dear Reader,

As a token of our appreciation for your interest in "*Buddhism for Beginners: Discover the Profound Wisdom of The Buddha's Teachings and Transform Your Life Through Zen Meditation And Mindfulness Practices,*" we are thrilled to offer you an exclusive bonus that will complement your journey towards mindfulness and inner peace.

Included with your purchase of this book is a special gift – 30 minutes of guided meditation, thoughtfully designed to enhance your meditation practice and bring tranquility to your daily life. This guided meditation session is crafted to help you deepen your understanding of mindfulness, cultivate a sense of serenity, and tap into the profound wisdom of the Buddha's teachings.

Meditation is a powerful tool that can lead to numerous benefits, including reduced stress, improved focus, heightened self-awareness, and an overall sense of well-being. Whether you are a beginner or an experienced meditator, this guided session will guide you on a path of inner exploration and personal growth.

BONUS INCLUDED: 30 MINUTES OF GUIDED MEDITATION

To access your bonus guided meditation, simply scan the QR code below, and let this transformative experience be your companion on your journey toward self-discovery and spiritual enlightenment.

We sincerely hope that this bonus offer enhances your reading experience and supports your commitment to cultivating mindfulness in your life. Your satisfaction is of utmost importance to us, and we believe this meditation gift will be a valuable addition to your practice.

Thank you for choosing "*Buddhism for Beginners*" and for being part of our community. May this book and the bonus guided meditation inspire you on your path to a more fulfilling and mindful existence.

With gratitude,

Samadhi Sands

ABOUT THE AUTHOR

Samadhi Sands was born and raised in a Buddhist family in northern California. He has been interested in meditation and spirituality since a young age, and began practicing Buddhism seriously in his early 20s. After completing his undergraduate studies in Religious Studies, he pursued a graduate degree in Buddhist Studies at a prominent university in the United States.

After completing his studies, Samadhi Sands spent several years living in Buddhist communities in Asia and Europe, deepening his understanding of the philosophy and practices of Buddhism. He spent many hours in silent meditation, and studied with several renowned Buddhist teachers during this time.

Eventually, Samadhi Sands returned to the United States and began writing about his experiences and insights as a Buddhist practitioner. His book, "Buddhism for Beginners," provides an accessible and comprehensive introduction to the principles and practices of Buddhism, with a particular focus on mindfulness meditation.

Samadhi Sands' writing has been well-received by both beginners and experienced practitioners, and his book has become a popular resource for those interested in learning more about Buddhism. In addition to his writing, Samadhi Sands continues to teach meditation and lead retreats, sharing his knowledge and experience with others who seek to deepen their spiritual practice.